Launch Your Notary Public and Loan Signing Agent Business

Earn Six Figures Working on Your Terms and Schedule

Alyssa and Garrett Garner

Disclaimer

***Note from the authors:** Below is the standard disclaimer that books like this typically include. To summarize in our own words, we would like you to know that starting or running a business of any kind comes with inherent risk. If you choose to take the leap, you alone are responsible for the actions and choices you make in your business. While we wish you all the success in the world, we can't make any guarantees that the steps outlined here will have any particular outcome for you, as results are based on many factors. Always consider your decisions carefully, while also maintaining a healthy dose of optimism!*

The information in this book is for informational and educational purposes only. It should not be construed as business, tax, or legal advice of any kind. All information and resources found in this book are based on the opinions of the authors alone unless otherwise noted.

The authors of this book assume no responsibility or liability for any consequence resulting directly or indirectly from any action or inaction you take based on the information found in this book.

Contents

Introduction

If you're reading this, you're likely exploring new opportunities in the business world. Perhaps you've grown weary of the traditional nine-to-five grind, are tired of punching the clock, or maybe you're an aspiring entrepreneur in search of a fresh challenge.

Whatever your reason, you are on the cusp of discovering a realistic pathway to financial independence, all while maintaining control over your schedule and your life.

This book is your gateway to launching your notary public and loan signing business—a venture that can put you on the path to financial success while granting you the freedom to dictate your working hours.

So, why wait? It's time to take the leap, embark on a journey where you craft your own paycheck, and unlock the doors to an exciting future.

Let's look at some of the reasons why you should seriously consider launching your own notary public and loan signing agent business:

Constant Demand for Notary and Loan Signing Services

Notary services are indispensable for a wide array of legal and financial transactions, from real estate purchases to wills, powers of attorney, and more. Similarly, loan signings are a necessity in the world of mortgage and refinancing transactions. The perpetual need for such services ensures a steady flow of potential customers at your doorstep.

Low Start-Up Cost

Starting a notary public and loan signing business typically comes with minimal initial expenses. Unlike many other businesses, you don't have to purchase retail inventory, hire a sizeable staff, or lease a large office space in order to get started. This low overhead empowers you to maximize your profits right from the beginning.

Flexible Working Hours

Notaries and loan signing agents often enjoy the luxury of setting their own working hours. You can effortlessly schedule appointments around your preexisting commitments, making it a perfect solution for those seeking to strike a harmonious balance between their work and personal lives. It is also an excellent source of supplementary income for those with other occupations.

Potential for Repeat Business

Many notary services and loan signings result in repeat business from the same clients, such as refinancing or repeated real estate transactions. Cultivating a loyal customer base will pave the way for a consistent income stream over the long term.

Opportunities for Expansion

You have the option to expand your business by providing mobile notary services, allowing you to travel to your clients' homes. You can even specialize in remote online notarizations, which would allow you to work from home, while potentially commanding higher fees. This ability to serve a broader clientele can significantly boost your income.

Competitive Pricing

Depending on your location, specialization, and expertise, you often have the flexibility to set competitive rates for your services. Loan signing agents, in particular, often charge fees per signing, which can translate into substantial income over time.

Seasonal Opportunities

While notary services are in demand throughout the year, certain seasons like spring and summer often experience heightened activity in the real estate market. These peak times can translate to larger earnings, adding extra appeal to this entrepreneurial venture.

Diversified Income Streams

In addition to notarization and loan signings, you can offer complementary services such as document preparation, mobile finger printing, or even wedding officiation, allowing you to diversify your income streams even further.

Tailor Your Income to Your Needs

Here is the beauty of this business: it is incredibly versatile. You can choose to work as little or as much as you prefer. If you aim to make $4,000 a month working part-time or as a side hustle, you can do just that. If you decide to go full-time, you could scale up to earning $20,000 or more per month. You hold the reins to your income; you quite literally write your own paycheck!

With the right attitude and dedication, your notary public and loan signing agent business can generate a profitable income while allowing you to work around your schedule and lifestyle.

Now that we've explored the many advantages of embarking on the journey of becoming a notary public and loan signing agent, let's take the first steps toward shaping your entrepreneurial destiny.

You have the vision, the knowledge, and the tools at your disposal —it's time to seize success, break free from the ordinary, and create a life where you are the author of your story!

The Basics

Before we get started, let's introduce the basics. In this section, we'll cover what a notary is, what a loan signing agent is, and the key differences between the two.

What Is a Notary?

Basic Definition

A notary is a public representative that the state government appoints to act as an objective witness in a variety of legal and financial transactions. Their major function is to discourage fraud by ensuring the correct identification of parties involved in the document, validating their willingness to sign, and confirming the document's legitimacy. To ensure the integrity of the notarization process, notaries are supposed to follow specified norms and regulations.

The primary types of notaries are as follows:

- Traditional notaries, who perform in-person notarization using pen and paper.
- Electronic notaries, who perform in-person notarization using digital technology and electronic signatures.
- Remote online notaries (RON), who perform remote notarization using online technology.

Who May Become a Notary in the United States?

The requirements for becoming a notary can vary according to which state you live or work in. However, there are some common requirements and steps that individuals typically need to follow to become notaries in the US. We'll look at all of these requirements in more detail in the following chapters.

Responsibilities of a Notary

- **Verification of identity:** Notaries are responsible for verifying the identity of the individuals signing the document. This typically means checking government-issued identification, such as a driver's license or passport.
- **Witnessing signatures:** Notaries witness the signing of documents and confirm that the parties involved are doing so willingly and under no duress.
- **Administering oaths and affirmations:** Notaries have the authority to administer oaths and affirmations, which are legally binding declarations of truthfulness. This is often required in affidavits and sworn statements.
- **Certifying copies:** Some notaries are authorized to certify copies of certain documents as true copies of the original.
- **Journal keeping:** Notaries are typically required to maintain a detailed journal of all notarized transactions,

including the names of the parties, the type of document, the date, and other pertinent information.

Benefits of Being a Notary

- Notaries charge fees for their services, which can provide a supplementary income stream or be a primary source of income for those who specialize in notary work. So, you get to decide what you want to earn and how much you need to work to achieve your goal.
- A big advantage is the fact that most notaries have flexible schedules and the ability to set their own working hours, making it an excellent option for a high-earning side hustle.
- If you already have a successful career in real estate, law, or banking, becoming a notary may give you an edge over your competitors.

Restrictions on Notaries

- **Geographical limitations:** Notaries are typically authorized to operate only within the state or jurisdiction where they are commissioned.
- **Conflict of interest:** Notaries must avoid any conflicts of interest in notarizing documents. They should avoid notarizing documents in which they have a personal interest.
- **Ineligible parties:** Certain individuals, such as those convicted of a felony, may be ineligible to become notaries in some states.
- **Prohibited acts:** Notaries are prohibited from engaging in any illegal or unethical conduct, including

notarizing documents without proper identification or consent.

- **Expiration and renewal:** Notary commissions have expiration dates, and notaries have to renew their commissions by meeting state-specific requirements.

What Is a Loan Signing Agent (LSA)?

Basic Definition

A loan signing agent (LSA) is a sort of notary public who has been trained and allowed to facilitate the signing of loan and mortgage documents on behalf of lenders, title companies, and borrowers during real estate transactions. LSAs play an important role in ensuring the accuracy of these documents and assisting in the smooth and efficient completion of loan closings.

Note that they may also be referred to as notary signing agents, or NSAs, but for the purpose of consistency, we will only refer to them as loan signing agents or LSAs throughout this book.

Who May Become a Loan Signing Agent in the United States?

To become an LSA in the US, individuals typically need to meet specific qualifications and requirements, which can vary from state to state. Before becoming an LSA, you must first be a commissioned notary public in your state.

Responsibilities of a Loan Signing Agent

- LSAs meticulously review loan and mortgage documents to ensure they are correctly prepared, accurately reflect the terms of the loan, and contain no errors or discrepancies.
- LSAs guide borrowers through the signing process, explaining the purpose of each document and ensuring

all necessary signatures, initials, and notarizations are completed accurately and in accordance with legal requirements.

- When necessary, LSAs administer oaths or affirmations to borrowers, making sure that they have a thorough understanding of the documents they are signing.
- LSAs act as impartial witnesses to the signing process, confirming that all parties willingly and knowingly execute the documents.
- As notary publics, LSAs also perform notarizations when required for certain documents within the loan package, such as affidavits or deeds of trust.
- After the signing is complete, LSAs are responsible for securely handling and returning the documents to the appropriate parties, like title companies or lenders.

Benefits of Being a Loan Signing Agent

- LSAs can earn substantial fees for each loan signing, making it a profitable career or side business.
- A huge benefit is the flexibility to choose their working hours and take on assignments that suit their availability, making it an excellent option for those seeking work-life balance.
- With a constant flow of real estate transactions, LSAs are consistently in high demand, providing a steady source of potential clients.
- Becoming an LSA allows notaries to specialize in a niche area of notary work, improving their expertise and marketability.

Restrictions on Loan Signing Agents

- LSAs are bound by the same laws and regulations as traditional notaries, including those related to conflicts of interest, ethics, and adherence to state-specific notary laws.
- LSAs should refrain from providing legal advice or interpreting the content of loan documents. Their role is strictly to facilitate the signing process.
- There can be certain restrictions on LSAs that vary by state. LSAs must always adhere to their state's specific regulations.

A career as a notary public and LSA offers not only financial opportunities but also the chance to play a vital role in the legal and financial systems. It is a profession that combines the satisfaction of helping individuals with the essential link in the real estate and lending industries, ensuring that transactions proceed smoothly and with integrity.

The trust and responsibility placed in you by clients and the community can be immensely fulfilling. So, if you are looking for a career path that combines flexibility, financial rewards, and the chance to make a meaningful impact, becoming a notary and LSA could be the exciting new endeavor you've been waiting for.

How This Book Works

Before we move onto the chapters themselves, we will first provide you with an overview of the three-part framework that forms the backbone of this book. Our goal is to guide you step by step, helping you turn your ambition into a thriving six-figure business.

Part I is called "Become a Notary Public and Loan Signing Agent." In this part, we will lay the foundation for your new career by focusing on the important first steps. You will discover how to become a notary public and learn the ropes of being a loan signing agent.

We will cover topics like these:

- **Understanding notary public basics:** You'll learn the exact steps for securing your notary commission, including legal prerequisites and state-by-state requirements.
- **Becoming a loan signing agent:** You will gain insight into the world of loan signings, what the

requirements are to become an LSA, and how to obtain your certification.

- **Your first appointment:** We will prepare you step-by-step to conduct your first notarization and signing appointment like a pro.
- **Stay in compliance:** You'll learn exactly what is needed to stay in compliance as a notary public and loan signing agent, including guidance for renewing your commission and certification, as well as maintaining a sterling professional reputation.

By the end of Part I, you'll have transformed from a novice into a skilled notary public and loan signing agent. You'll be ready to take on your first clients and start building your reputation in the industry. You'll feel confident, knowledgeable, and prepared to embark on this exciting new journey.

Part II is called "Start and Promote Your Business," and is about turning your newfound skills into a profitable venture. We'll provide you with the tools and strategies to start and promote your notary and loan signing business.

We will look at the following:

- **Getting your first client:** Discover actionable steps and strategies to secure your very first client within 24 hours of launching your business. We will help you kick-start your journey with confidence.
- **Six-figure marketing:** Learn the secrets of effective promotion and branding to attract a steady stream of clients. We will explore a variety of powerful marketing strategies that will catapult your income to the next level.
- **Should you form an LLC?** Weigh the pros and cons of forming a limited liability company (LLC) for your

business. We will guide you through the process of establishing your business entity, from choosing a business name to registering it with the proper authorities.

- **Taxes and insurance:** Navigate the often-confusing world of business taxes and insurance. We will provide essential insights on how to effectively manage your taxes and protect your business with the right insurance coverage.
- **Troubleshooting:** Understand common challenges that those who are new to this business often face. We will share valuable insights on avoiding pitfalls, resolving issues, and staying on the path to success.

As you progress through Part II, you'll go from being an enthusiastic newcomer to a confident business owner. You'll have your own notary and loan signing business up and running with a solid marketing plan in place.

You will feel a sense of accomplishment as clients begin to contact you for assistance, and you'll be well on your way to achieving financial independence. We will also help you prepare for any challenges that may come your way, making the road to success a smooth one.

Part III is called "Expand Your Business to Six Figures," and here we will help you take your business to the next level by achieving a six-figure income.

We will delve into advanced strategies for growth and income optimization, including these:

- **Diversification:** Explore opportunities to diversify your income streams and boost your earnings. We will discuss offering additional services like delivering documents, officiating weddings, or becoming an apostille agent that can significantly increase your bottom line.

- **Scaling to six figures:** Gain insights into how to scale your business efficiently to reach that coveted six-figure income mark without significantly increasing your workload. We will guide you in becoming a mobile notary, working with escrow officers, and working from home as a remote online notary or RON.
- **Long-term success:** Unlock the secrets of lasting success in the notary public and loan signing agent industries. You will learn the five must-know actions that, when practiced consistently, will result in a sustainable and lucrative business.

By the end of Part III, you will have achieved your goal of building a notary and loan signing business that generates a six-figure income. You'll experience the freedom that comes with financial security, and you'll have the flexibility to work on your own terms and decide your own schedule.

Imagine the sense of fulfillment and financial stability as you ascend to this impressive milestone in your notary and loan signing business. Your journey from a novice to a successful entrepreneur will be complete, and the exciting opportunities that await you will be yours to seize.

Part One

Become a Notary Public and Loan Signing Agent

Chapter 1

Become a Notary Public

Welcome to the first step on your path to becoming a notary public! In this chapter, we'll look at the most important aspects of becoming a notary, demystify the process, and equip you with the knowledge you need to get started on this exciting journey.

Becoming a notary public is more than just a legal destination; it's also the beginning of a versatile career. The pages that follow will teach you about the qualifications and requirements for becoming a notary public in each state.

By the end of this chapter, you'll have the motivation and know-how to take the first step toward a rewarding career as a notary public. So, let's get started and learn how to turn your dreams into reality.

Basic Requirements

First, let's lay the groundwork by looking at the fundamental criteria for becoming a notary public in the United States.

These are the general requirements that all states share:

- **Age requirement:** To be eligible for a notary public commission in any of the 50 states, you must be at least 18 years old. This age requirement ensures that notaries possess the maturity and legal capacity to fulfill their duties and responsibilities.
- **US citizenship and legal residency:** While most states don't require US citizenship, you must generally be a legal resident of the United States to become a notary public. Some states may have residency or immigration status requirements as well.
- **Clean criminal record:** Aspiring notaries must keep their criminal records clean. Many states conduct background checks on applicants to ensure that they have not been convicted of disqualifying crimes such as felonies or crimes of moral wrongdoing. During the application process, any prior criminal history should be disclosed.
- **Basic education:** While a high school diploma or equivalent is usually sufficient to start, many states require or recommend additional training for notary publics.
- **Residence in the commissioning state:** You must usually live in the state where you want to become a notary public. There are some states, however, that permit nonresidents to apply for commissions if they work or conduct business within the state.
- **Legal competence:** In order to enter into contracts and assume legal responsibilities, you must be legally competent to carry out your duties as a notary public.

These fundamental requirements serve as a national foundation for notary public commissions across the country.

Keep in mind that while these criteria apply broadly, specific state-by-state requirements can vary greatly. As we progress through this chapter, we will provide you with detailed information on the specific requirements and procedures that apply in your state, allowing you to confidently navigate the path to becoming a notary public.

The Process

In this section, we'll walk you through the basics of becoming a notary public, offering you a road map to get started. While the process can vary a bit from state to state, it will generally align with the guidelines below.

Determine Your Eligibility

Before you start on the journey to become a notary, make sure that you meet the basic eligibility requirements for your state, like age, citizenship, and residency. We have discussed the federal requirements above and will look in more detail at the requirements for each state later in this chapter.

Enroll in a Training Course

While not all states require formal training, it is strongly advised to take a notary training course. These courses offer valuable insights into notary laws, best practices, and the role's responsibilities.

Even if it is not required, training can help you become a more knowledgeable and effective notary. Most notary training courses are easily accessible online.

Obtain a Surety Bond

Many states require notaries to obtain a surety bond as a form of insurance to protect the public in the event of mistakes or misconduct during notarization. The bond amount varies from state to state.

Begin by choosing a reputable surety bond provider or insurance company licensed to issue notary bonds in your state. Depending on your state's requirements and the bond provider's policies, you may need to undergo a credit check to determine your eligibility for the bond. Once your application is approved, you will receive a bond certificate from the provider.

Most states require notaries to file their surety bond with the appropriate government authority, such as the Secretary of State's office or another designated agency. The filing ensures that the bond is on record and that you are in compliance with state regulations. Keep in mind that your surety bond should be renewed annually or as required by your state.

Complete the Application

Fill out the notary application provided by your state's notary commissioning authority (usually the Secretary of State's office). Prepare to provide personal information, surety bond details, and any necessary documentation.

Complete a Background Check (If Required)

To ensure that applicants have a clean criminal record, some states may require a background check or fingerprinting as part of the application process.

Take the Oath of Office

Following the approval of your application, you will be required to take an oath of office, swearing to uphold the duties and responsibilities of a notary public.

Receive Your Certificate of Notary Commission

You will receive your notary commission once all requirements have been met, indicating that you are an authorized notary public in your state.

Obtain Errors and Omissions (E&O) Insurance

While not required in all states, it is strongly recommended that notaries consider errors and omissions (E&O) insurance. This insurance covers notaries for mistakes or oversights made during notarizations. We will discuss E&O insurance in more detail in Chapter 8.

Obtain Your Notary Stamp

You will need to obtain a notary stamp or seal, which is an important tool for notarizing documents. Your name, commission expiration date, and other required information are typically included on the stamp.

Cost and Time

The cost, processing time, and amount of time to become a notary public can vary greatly depending on your state.

Below, we provide general estimates to give you an idea of what to expect:

Cost

- **Application fee:** For notary commissions, most states charge an application fee. Depending on the state, this fee can range between $10 and $75 or more.
- **Training course (if required):** If your state requires notary training, you may be required to pay for a training course, which can range between $100 and $200 on average.

- **Surety bond:** Notaries are frequently required to obtain a surety bond, which can cost between $50 and $200 per year, depending on your state's bond requirement.
- **Notary stamp or seal:** The cost of a notary stamp or seal varies, but is typically between $20 and $50.
- **Additional materials:** You will often need supplies as a notary public, such as a journal and printer. The cost of these can vary greatly, but can generally amount to $100 to $300 or more.

Processing Time

Processing times for notary applications can vary widely. In some states, you may receive your commission certificate within a few weeks, while in others, it may take several months. Generally, it is a good idea to plan for a processing time of one to three months.

Time Investment

The time you will need to devote to the notary application process will vary depending on factors such as your state's requirements, the time it takes to complete any required training, and how quickly your application is processed.

In general, you can expect to spend between 10 and 30 hours preparing your application, attending training (if necessary), and completing the required steps.

If you need your commission sooner, some states charge a fee for expedited processing.

Supplies

Certain supplies and materials will be required to perform notarizations effectively and in accordance with your state's regulations.

The following is a general list of supplies that are commonly required for notary work:

Notary Stamp or Seal

When notarizing documents, a notary stamp or seal is essential. The design and specifications of the stamp may differ from one state to the next.

Notaries can obtain their official notary stamp or seal from a number of sources, depending on their state's regulations and preferences. These may include office supply stores, notary supply companies, and online retailers specializing in notary supplies.

Record Book or Journal

Many states require notaries to keep a notary record book or journal in which they record the details of each notarization they perform. This journal serves as a record and can help protect you in cases of dispute or other legal issues.

Printer

As you will need to print documents that require notarization, a printer is an essential piece of equipment for your business. We recommend a dual tray laser printer that is equipped for both legal and letter-sized paper. While a new one can be a bit pricey, ranging from $200 to $300 or more, you can often find a used one on eBay for a fraction of the price.

Ink Pad

Some states may require notaries to use an ink pad with their stamp or seal to create a physical ink impression on documents. You will need to check your state's regulations to see if this is required where you reside.

Notary Certificate Forms

Notary certificate forms are often necessary for notarizing specific types of documents. These forms may include acknowledgment certificates, jurat certificates, or other state-specific certificates.

Identification Tools

You may need to have tools like a magnifying glass or ultraviolet (UV) light to help verify the authenticity of identification documents presented by individuals whose signatures you notarize.

Seal Embosser (If Applicable)

Some states allow notaries to use a seal embosser in addition to or instead of a stamp. Check your state's laws to see if a seal embosser is required or optional.

To find out more about the specific supply requirements for your state, including any unique regulations or additional materials required, you can check out your Secretary of State's website or visit asnnotary.org/?form=supplies.

State-By-State Requirements

This section will provide a comprehensive overview of notary regulations across all 50 states plus Washington, DC. Feel free to skip ahead to the section dedicated to your state to access the exact guidelines that apply to your jurisdiction.

You can find the most up-to-date requirements at asnnotary.org/?form=stateinfo as well as on your Secretary of State's website.

Alabama

The requirements vary from county to county. It is best to contact a probate judge in your county for the specific requirements. Training is required for all applicants who are not attorneys. The notary bond requirement is $50,000 for the four-year term.

Alaska

Notary applicants must be at least 18 years old and be residents of Alaska. They should not have been in prison or convicted of a felony during the 10 years before applying. There is no training or exam required. The notary bond requirement is $2,500 for the four-year term.

Arizona

Notary applicants must be at least 18 years old and be residents of Arizona. They should be fluent (reading and writing) in English, be a US citizen or a legal permanent resident, and not been convicted of a felony. No training or exams are required under most circumstances. The notary bond requirement is $5,000 for the four-year term.

Arkansas

Notary applicants must be at least 18 years old, be a resident of Arkansas or one of its bordering states, and be fluent in English (reading and writing). Applicants should not have had a commission revoked within 10 years from the date of applying and not been convicted of a felony. Training and an exam are required for electronic notaries while traditional notaries only need to pass an exam successfully. The notary bond requirement is $7,500 for the 10-year term.

California

Notary applicants must be at least 18 years old and be residents of California. They have to complete a state-approved education course and pass a written exam. The state also requires a clear background check. The notary bond requirement is $15,000 for the four-year term.

Colorado

Notary applicants must be at least 18 years old, be a resident of Colorado, or be employed within the state. Additionally, applicants need to be US citizens or legal residents of the US and be fluent in English (reading and writing). An education course and exam is required for new and renewing notaries. There is no notary bond requirement for the four-year term.

Connecticut

Notary applicants must be at least 18 years old and be residents of Connecticut or be employed within the state. An exam is required for new and renewing notaries, but no notary bond is required for the five-year term.

Delaware

Notary applicants must be at least 18 years old, and be legal residents of the state. Those employed within the state with a physical business address may also apply. The applicants should also be of good character and have a reasonable need for a commission. There is no notary bond required, and terms of office vary between two and four years, depending on the type of commission.

District of Columbia

Notary applicants must be at least 18 years old and be legal residents or citizens of the US. They also need to work or live within the district. Once an application is approved, the notary needs to attend an orientation by the mayor. The notary bond requirement is $2,000 for the five-year term.

Florida

Notary applicants must be at least 18 years old and be residents of the state. They should also be fluent in English (understanding, reading, and writing). Applicants should report any criminal charges, even if they were not convicted, on the notary application. Applicants applying for the first time, also need to complete an approved three-hour notary education course. The notary bond requirement is $7,500 for the four-year term.

Georgia

Notary applicants must be at least 18 years old and be legal residents or citizens of the US. They must also be legal residents in the county in which they are applying. Applicants need to have an operating phone number which must be provided at the time of the application. No notary education, exam, or bond is required and the term of office is four years.

Hawaii

Notary applicants must be at least 18 years old and be residents of the state. They also need to meet the other qualifications required of public officers in Hawaii, including being a US citizen. Applicants need to complete and pass a notary exam, and a $1,000 bond is required for the four-year term.

Idaho

Notary applicants must be at least 18 years old and be citizens or permanent residents of the US, as well as residents of Idaho. They should also be fluent in English (reading and writing). No training or exam is required. The notary bond requirement is $10,000 for the six-year term.

Illinois

Notary applicants must be at least 18 years old and have been residents of the state for at least 30 days. They should also be citizens or permanent residents of the US. Applicants should be fluent in English (reading and writing) and not been convicted of a felony. Furthermore, they should not have had a notary commission suspended in the past 10 years. There is no training or exam requirement, and a notary bond of $5,000 is required for the four-year term.

Indiana

Notary applicants must be at least 18 years old and be residents of the state or primarily employed within the state. Notary education and an exam are required for new and renewing notaries, and continuing education is required every two years while the commission is active. The notary bond requirement is $25,000 for an eight-year term.

Iowa

Notary applicants must be at least 18 years old and be citizens or permanent residents of the US. They should also be residents of Iowa or residents of a bordering state who are employed in Iowa. Initial training is required for traditional notaries, while additional training may be required for remote online notaries. There is no notary bond required. The term length is three years for Iowa residents and one year for nonresidents.

Kansas

Notary applicants must be at least 18 years old and live or work in Kansas. Only electronic notaries need notary training. A notary bond of $12,000 is required for the four-year term.

Kentucky

Notary applicants must be at least 18 years old and be citizens or permanent legal residents of the US and be fluent in English (reading and writing). The applicant should also be a resident of the state or have a place of employment in Kentucky and not be disqualified under the Kentucky Revised Statutes 423.395. The state does not require notary education or exams but does require a $1,000 notary bond for the four-year commission term.

Louisiana

Applicants should be at least 18 years old and be residents of the state. They should also be registered to vote in the parish where they are applying and not have been convicted or pardoned of a felony. Applicants must be fluent in English (speaking, reading, and writing) and have a high school diploma or equivalent. The state requires a pre-assessment exam and state exam but state-licensed attorneys are exempt from taking the exam. This is a life-long commission with a $10,000 notary bond or errors and omissions coverage renewable every five years.

Maine

Applicants should be at least 18 years old and be proficient in English. They should be a resident of Maine or a resident of New Hampshire who is regularly employed in Maine. The applicant should be recommended for the commission by a registered Maine voter and not have a notary commission revoked in the state of Maine or any other state within five years of applying. Applicants should also not have been convicted of and imprisoned for a crime. There is an exam required for first-time applicants while renewing applicants take the exam via the Total Notary Solution-Online Renewal system. There is no requirement for a notary bond. The term length is seven years for Maine residents and three years for New Hampshire residents.

Maryland

Notary applicants should be at least 18 years old and be residents of the state or regularly employed in the state. Applicants should be of good moral character and able to perform the duties required of them. Training consists of a course of study and an exam for new applicants and refresher courses for renewing applicants. There is no notary bond requirement for the four-year term.

Massachusetts

Applicants should be at least 18 years old and live in the state or conduct business on a regular basis in the state. There is no training or exam requirement. No bond is required for the seven-year term of the commission.

Michigan

Applicants must be at least 18 years old and fluent in English (reading and writing), as well as residents of the state or have a place of business in the state. They should be American citizens or have proof of legal presence. They should also be a resident of the county in which they are applying. Applicants should not have been convicted of a felony in the 10 years prior to applying or convicted of two or more misdemeanor offenses involving the Michigan Notary Public Act within the 12-month period while commissioned. There are no requirements for education or an exam, but a $10,000 notary bond is required for the six to seven-year term of the commission.

Minnesota

Notary applicants must be at least 18 years old and residents of the state or residents of a county in Iowa, North Dakota, South Dakota, or Wisconsin. Training is not required for new or renewing notaries, but a list of entities that offer a course of study for a Minnesota remote online notary is available from the Secretary of State. No notary bond is required for the five-year term.

Mississippi

Applicants should be 18 years or older and fluent in English (reading and writing). They should be a resident of the state and have resided in the county of their residence for at least 30 days before the application is submitted. They should be a citizen or legal resident of the United States and not have been convicted of a felony, not have been incarcerated, or be on probation or parole. There is no requirement for training or exams, but a $5,000 notary bond is required for the four-year term.

Missouri

Notary applicants need to be at least 18 years old and fluent in English (reading and writing). They should be a registered voter in the county in which they are applying or be a permanent resident of the US. Applicants should not have had a notary commission revoked within the past 10 years. Nonresidents of the state may apply if they are employed in Missouri and can provide a work address in the county they are applying in, and plan to use the notary commission for their work only. Training or self-study of the Missouri Notary Handbook and an exam are required for new and returning applicants. There is a $10,000 notary bond requirement for the four-year term.

Montana

Notary applicants must be 18 years or older and be citizens or permanent residents of the US. They should also be a resident of Montana or have a place of business, be regularly employed, hold a valid professional license, or be the spouse or legal dependent of military personnel assigned to active duty in Montana. Education and an exam are required for new and renewing traditional notaries, as well as electronic notaries and remote online notaries. There is a $25,000 bond requirement for the four-year term of the commission.

Nebraska

Applicants must be at least 19 years old and be residents of Nebraska or residents of a bordering state and employed regularly in Nebraska. They should not have been convicted of a felony or a crime involving dishonesty or fraud in the past five years. New traditional and electronic notaries need to take and pass a written exam. There is a $15,000 bond requirement for the four-year term.

Nevada

Applicants should be at least 18 years old and be a resident of the state. They must not have committed a felony or have had a commission revoked in another state. Nonresidents living in bordering states may apply for a nonresident notary commission as long as they are regularly employed in the state of Nevada. All new and renewing notaries (traditional, electronic, and remote) need to complete training and pass an exam. There is a $10,000 bond requirement for the four-year term.

New Hampshire

Notary applicants must be at least 18 years old. They should be a resident of the state or resident of a bordering state who has primary employment in New Hampshire and is also a registered notary public in their state of residence. Applicants are also required to sign a written statement under oath as to whether they have ever been convicted of a crime that has not been annulled by a court. This does not include minor traffic violations. Applicants also need to have an endorsement by two notaries and one registered voter of New Hampshire. There is no education or exam requirement, and also no notary bond requirement for the five-year term.

New Jersey

Applicants must be at least 18 years old and be a resident of the state or a bordering state and be regularly employed in the state of New Jersey. They should not have been convicted of a crime anywhere in the US of the first or second degree, or an offense of dishonesty. There is an education and exam requirement for new applicants and continuing education for renewing notaries (attorneys are exempt from this requirement). There is no notary bond requirement for the five-year term.

New Mexico

Applicants should be 18 years or older and be a resident of the state. They should be fluent in English (reading and writing) and not have pleaded guilty to a felony nor been convicted of one. They should also not have had a notary commission revoked in the past 5 years prior to applying. There is an education and exam requirement for new notaries or renewing notaries who have been without a commission for more than one year. There is a notary bond requirement of $10,000 for the four-year term.

New York

Notary applicants should be at least 18 years old and be a resident of the state or have an office or place of business in the state. They should not have been convicted of a felony or any specified misdemeanors. Applicants should pass the New York State notary exam, though New York attorneys and court clerks of the Unified Court System are exempt from the examination. Renewing notaries must take the exam if commission has lapsed for more than six months. There is no notary bond requirement for the four-year term.

North Carolina

Applicants must be at least 18 years old, be fluent in English (reading and writing), and reside legally in the US. They should be a resident of North Carolina or be regularly employed in the state.

Applicants should possess a high school diploma or equivalent. They are also required to purchase and keep a current copy of the manual approved by the Secretary of State that describes the duties and authority of notaries. First-time applicants need to complete an education course and successfully complete an exam. There is also an education and exam requirement for electronic notaries. Members of the North Carolina State Bar are exempted from traditional notary education and exams. There is no notary bond requirement for the five-year term of commission.

North Dakota

Notary applicants must be at least 18 years old and fluent in English (reading and writing). They should be a citizen or permanent legal resident of the US and be a resident of the state of North Dakota. Nonresidents who have a place of employment in the state or reside in certain counties that border the state may also apply. There are no notary education or exam requirements, but there is a $7,500 bond requirement for the four-year term.

Ohio

Applicants should be at least 18 years old and be a legal resident of Ohio or an attorney who has their primary practice in the state. Applicants should not be disqualified from receiving a commission and not have been convicted or pleaded guilty to a disqualifying offense. There is an exam required for new and renewing notaries. Ohio attorneys are exempted from the exam requirement but have to complete the education component. There is also an exam requirement for online notary publics. There is no notary bond requirement for the five-year term.

Oklahoma

Applicants must be at least 18 years old and be a resident of the state or a bordering state who is regularly employed within Oklahoma. Applicants should be fluent in English (reading and writing) and not have been convicted of a felony. There is no education or exam requirement, but a $1,000 notary bond is required for the four-year term.

Oregon

Notary applicants should be at least 18 years old and be a resident of the state or have regular employment or practice in the state. They should be fluent in English (reading and writing) and not have had a notary commission revoked within 10 years of the date of applying. They should not have been convicted of a felony or a crime involving fraud, dishonesty, or deceit within the past 10 years. They should also not have been found by a court to have practiced law without a license or engaged in an unlawful trade practice. There is an education course and exam requirement for new applicants or renewing notaries whose commissions will lapse before renewal should be completed. There is no notary bond requirement for the four-year term.

Pennsylvania

Notary applicants must be 18 years or older and be a citizen or permanent legal resident of the US. They should be a resident of Pennsylvania or have a place of employment or practice in the state. They should be fluent in English (reading and writing) and not be disqualified from receiving a commission due to character, criminal convictions, or prior sanctions. There is an education and exam requirement for new and renewing notary applicants. A $10,000 notary bond is required for the four-year term.

Rhode Island

Applicants must be at least 18 years old and be permanent legal residents or citizens of the US. They should also be residents of Rhode Island or be employed or have a practice within the state.

Applicants should be fluent in English and not be disqualified under the Uniform Law on Notarial Acts. There are no education requirements but an applicant must demonstrate the necessary knowledge of Rhode Island's notary laws through passing an exam. There is no notary bond requirement for the four-year term.

South Carolina

Notary applicants must be registered to vote and able to read and write in English. There are no education or exam requirements and no notary bond is required for the 10-year term.

South Dakota

Notary applicants must be a resident of the state of South Dakota or a resident of a bordering county and regularly employed in the state. Applicants should not have been convicted of a felony. There is no education or exam required. The notary bond requirement is $5,000 for the six-year term.

Tennessee

Applicants must be at least 18 years old and be a citizen or legal permanent resident of the US. They should also be a resident of the state or be regularly employed within the state. Applicants should not have had a notary commission revoked for official misconduct in Tennessee or any other state. There is no education or exam requirement, but a $10,000 notary bond is required for the four-year term.

Texas

Notary applicants must be at least 18 years old and a resident of Texas. Nonresidents living in New Mexico, Oklahoma, Arkansas, or Louisiana who have qualified as a Texas escrow officer are also eligible for appointment as a Texas traditional notary public. Applicants should also not have a conviction for a crime involving moral turpitude or a felony that has not been set aside. There is no education requirement but there may be special circumstances where the Secretary of State will require additional training. There is a notary bond requirement of $10,000 for the four-year term of the commission.

Utah

Applicants must be 18 years or older and be a US citizen or have permanent resident status. They should have been a resident of the state for 30 days prior to the application being submitted. Applicants should be fluent in English (reading, writing, and understanding). Applicants have to submit to a mandatory background check. There is an online exam requirement for new and renewing notaries. A notary bond of $5,000 is required for the four-year commission term and additional bond limits are required for remote online notaries.

Vermont

Notary applicants should be at least 18 years old, be a citizen or permanent legal resident of the US, and be a resident of the state of Vermont or have a place of employment or practice in the state. An exam is required for new applicants while renewing notaries need to complete two hours of continuing education. There are no notary bond requirements for the two-year term.

Virginia

Applicants must be at least 18 years old and fluent in English (reading and writing) and be a legal resident of the US. Applicants should also live or work in the Commonwealth of Virginia and not have been convicted of a felony. There is no education or exam requirement and no notary bond is required for the four-year term.

Washington

Notary applicants should be at least 18 years old and fluent in English (reading and writing). They should be a citizen or permanent legal resident of the US and live in the state or have a place of employment or practice in the state. There is no education or exam requirement and a $10,000 notary bond is required for the four-year term of commission.

West Virginia

Applicants should be at least 18 years old and be a citizen or permanent legal resident of the US. They should also be a resident of the state or be employed in the state of West Virginia. They should have a high school diploma or equivalent and be fluent in English (reading and writing). There is no education or exam requirement and no notary bond is required for the five-year term.

Wisconsin

Notary applicants should be at least 18 years old and be a resident of the US with at least an eighth-grade education. They need to demonstrate adherence to the laws of the state with regard to arrests and convictions. There is no education requirement for traditional notaries but applicants need to pass the notary exam with at least 90%. Training is required for remote online notaries. There is a $500 notary bond requirement for the four-year term.

Wyoming

Applicants must be at least 18 years old and be citizens or permanent legal residents of the US. They should also be a resident of the state, employed within the state, or a legal dependent of military personnel assigned to active duty within the state. Applicants are required to take the notary education presentation provided by the state and take an exam. There is no notary bond requirement for the six-year term.

Chapter 2

Become a Loan Signing Agent

Once you are officially a notary public, you can pursue your loan signing agent certification. By combining both roles, you'll diversify your revenue streams to earn an even bigger income!

The real estate industry is a constant source of loan signings, offering LSAs a steady flow of assignments. Developing relationships with local title companies, lenders, and signing services as an LSA can also benefit your notary business, as these connections can lead to additional notary assignments. This can help you to establish a reliable base and six-figure income.

In this chapter, we'll show you how to harness your skills and ambition to embark on a career that not only promises financial success but also provides you with the keys to a world of opportunity. Are you ready to turn your dreams into reality and take control of your future as a loan signing agent?

Basic Requirements

First, you should have a current notary public commission in a state that does not prohibit signing agent activity.

When you apply, a background check will be done, and applicants need to meet the standards of the Signing Professionals Workgroup (SPW). Applicants should note that an annual background check is needed to be an LSA.

Applicants may need to complete a training course covering the duties, responsibilities, and limitations of a loan signing agent.

The Process

Below is the general process for becoming a loan signing agent.

Complete Loan Signing Agent Training

While not all states require formal training for LSAs, it is highly recommended to undergo specialized training to understand loan document procedures, signing protocols, and industry best practices.

Training courses are widely available online and in person through reputable organizations like the National Notary Association (NNA) and the Loan Signing System.

Training typically covers topics such as:

- loan document types and terminology.
- proper notarization procedures for loan documents.
- signing agent responsibilities and ethics.
- how to handle common loan document issues.

Apply for Certification

The Signing Professionals Workgroup (SPW) oversees the certification process. Many lenders and signing services require certification from SPW, so getting this will help you qualify for more jobs and give you legitimacy in the industry.

The process for certification is as follows:

- Pass an SPW-compliant exam (you need a score of 80% or higher).
- Pass an SPW-compliant background check.
- Purchase E&O insurance.

Our top recommendation for becoming a certified loan signing agent is through the National Notary Association (NNA). They have a package that includes a training course, an exam, and a background check. Please note that they refer to this as a notary signing agent certification, but it's the same thing as a loan signing agent certification.

Cost and Time

Cost

- **Training course:** The cost of a loan signing agent training course typically ranges from $100 to $300. Some courses may include additional study materials or resources in their fees.
- **Errors and Omissions (E&O) Insurance:** E&O insurance premiums for LSAs vary based on coverage limits and other factors. On average, you can expect to pay between $200 and $400 annually for E&O insurance.
- **Supplies and equipment:** This may include costs for paper, ink, office supplies, and more. Most of these

materials will overlap with the ones already needed for your notary public business.

Time

- **Training:** Most loan signing agent training courses can be completed in a matter of days or weeks, depending on your schedule and the course's format (online or in person).
- **E&O insurance:** Obtaining E&O insurance can typically be done in a relatively short period of time, with the application and approval process often taking a few days to a few weeks.
- **Market preparation:** Building your online presence, networking with industry professionals, and marketing your LSA services can be an ongoing effort that may take several months to establish.
- **Performing loan signings:** Once you are certified and ready to work, the time spent on loan signings will vary depending on the number of assignments you take on and your availability.

Supplies and Equipment

As an LSA, you will need specific supplies and equipment, including:

- a notary stamp or seal.
- a high-quality laser printer for printing loan documents.
- a computer with internet access for communication with clients and document retrieval.
- basic office supplies such as pens, paper, and a dedicated workspace.

You'll likely have already obtained most, if not all, of these supplies for your notary public business, making the expansion to an LSA business relatively easy and seamless.

State Restrictions

Many loan signing services are performed at real estate closings. While most states don't have restrictions on this, some do have additional requirements or limitations related specifically to real estate closings.

We will address these restrictions in the following section. For the most up-to-date information on your state's specific requirements, you can visit <u>nationalnotary.org/support/signing-agents/state-restrictions.</u>

Connecticut

Connecticut law does not allow for persons who are not Connecticut attorneys (including out-of-state attorneys) to conduct closings for most mortgage loan transactions.

Delaware

The closing of a real estate or refinance transaction may only be conducted by a Delaware attorney.

Georgia

The closing of a real estate transaction is viewed as a practice of law and requires a Georgia attorney to be present or involved in the closing.

Indiana

Indiana law requires anyone who conducts a real estate closing to hold a professional insurance producer license.

Maryland

Maryland law requires a professional insurance producer license to conduct real estate closings.

Massachusetts

Massachusetts law requires an attorney to conduct a real estate closing; a non-attorney notary who is employed by the lender may, however, notarize the document in conjunction with the closing of the employer's real estate loan.

Minnesota

Any person conducting a real estate closing in the state must hold a closing agent license.

Nebraska

Notaries are not allowed to charge more than the maximum fee for a notarial act and the per-mile travel costs authorized for government employees.

Nevada

Nevada statutes limit the fees notaries are allowed to charge for notarial acts as well as travel.

New York

Some parts of the state require an attorney to conduct the closing of real estate transactions. As a result, certain companies only provide assignments to licensed attorneys.

New York property law requires both the lender and mortgagor of a reverse mortgage loan to be represented by an attorney at the time of closing.

North Carolina

Notaries are allowed to provide loan signing services at a real estate closing, but oversight and supervision by an attorney are required.

South Carolina

A South Carolina attorney needs to supervise and conduct a real estate closing.

Texas

Home equity line of credit (HELOC) loans may only be signed and closed at the permanent physical address of a lender, Texas attorney, or title company.

Vermont

An attorney needs to be present or involved in a real estate closing. A paralegal is allowed to conduct a loan closing if the paralegal's role is administrative and under the supervision of an attorney.

Virginia

The Virginia Bureau of Insurance requires anyone who conducts a real estate closing to hold a title insurance license if they receive or handle money for closing costs.

West Virginia

An attorney needs to conduct a real estate closing, as the transaction is considered a practice of law.

As we conclude this chapter, keep in mind that the path you are choosing in becoming a loan signing agent is a journey toward financial freedom, personal empowerment, and limitless prospects.

You are not only signing documents when you become an LSA; you are also signing your own future. You are on the cusp of establishing a flourishing business that provides not just a considerable income but also the flexibility to live life on your own terms.

So, embrace the challenges, celebrate the successes, and continue to develop your skills and knowledge. You will soon discover that being an LSA is not just a job; it is a fulfilling career that allows you to make a difference in the lives of others while simultaneously earning a six-figure income.

We want to encourage you to take the leap of faith, follow your passion, and let the journey to becoming an LSA inspire you to achieve your dreams. The possibilities are endless, and the future is yours to shape.

Chapter 3

Your First Appointment

It is never too late to be what you might have been. –George Eliot

Congratulations on taking your first steps as a notary public and loan signing agent! Your journey has led you to this exciting moment—the moment of your first appointment.

It's natural to feel a mix of anticipation and enthusiasm, and perhaps a touch of nervousness. But fear not, because in this chapter, we'll guide you through every step, ensuring that your first appointment is a huge success.

Whether you're notarizing a simple document or a complex legal agreement, we're here to help you prepare. We'll discuss fees, how to get paid (woo-hoo!), and the step-by-step process for conducting your first notarization or signing appointment like a pro. So, take a deep breath, and let's go!

Fees

Notary Public Fees

State governments typically set notary public fees and regulate them to prevent unfair pricing and ensure that they are affordable for the general public. These fees can vary greatly from one state to the next.

Notaries may charge a fee up to the maximum permitted by their state's fee schedule. While you may charge travel costs, the signer must agree to it in advance.

Common notary duties that can incur set fees include the following:

- **Acknowledgments:** Notarizing acknowledgments, which verify the signer's voluntary acknowledgment of their signature, often has a set fee per acknowledgement or per signature notarized.
- **Jurats:** Notarizing jurats, which require the signer to swear or affirm the truth of the document's content, may have a fee based on the number of signatures or pages involved.
- **Travel fees:** Notaries may charge additional fees for traveling to the signer's location, especially for mobile notary services. These fees are usually per trip and can vary widely.
- **Copy certification:** If a notary is asked to certify a copy of an original document, there may be a set fee per copy certified.
- **Oath or affirmation:** Administering an oath or affirmation, which can be required for various documents, may have a set fee.

- **Miscellaneous fees:** Some states allow notaries to charge additional fees for services like witnessing document signings, providing witness signatures, or notarizing protests or depositions.

To get a better idea of the current notary fees in your state, you can visit nationalnotary.org/knowledge-center/about-notaries/notary-fees-by-state.

Loan Signing Agent Fees

Loan signing agents typically have more flexibility in setting their fees, and their rates can vary based on factors such as location, complexity of the loan package, and the LSA's experience.

While LSAs should ensure that their fees are reasonable and competitive, they may charge for the following services:

- **Loan signings:** Fees for loan signings can vary widely based on the type and size of the loan package. LSAs often charge a flat fee for standard loan signings, which includes printing, traveling, and notarization services.
- **Additional services:** LSAs may charge extra for services like traveling long distances, accommodating last-minute appointments, or handling more complex loan packages.
- **Cancellations and no-shows:** Many LSAs have cancellation policies that allow them to charge a fee if a signing is canceled or if the signer does not show up for the appointment.
- **Print and delivery fees:** Some LSAs charge additional fees for printing documents and delivering them to the signing location.

It's important for both notaries and LSAs to be transparent about their fees and to adhere to all relevant state regulations. Notaries must always comply with their state's fee schedule, while LSAs can set their fees within the bounds of their local market and competitive pricing practices.

Getting Paid

Payment for Notaries

Notaries typically receive payment at the time of service. When someone requires notarization of a document, they pay the notary directly for the services rendered.

Payment methods can vary and may include cash, checks, or other forms of electronic payment. The notary may provide a receipt that shows proof of the notarization and payment for the service.

Payment for Loan Signing Agents

Loan signing agents often operate as independent contractors or as part of signing services that facilitate loan signings for lenders, title companies, or escrow companies. The payment process for LSAs differs from that of traditional notaries.

- **Invoice submission:** After completing a loan signing appointment, LSAs typically submit an invoice to the signing service or hiring entity. This invoice outlines the services provided, including the type of loan package, date of the signing, location, and any additional services performed.
- **Billing period:** LSAs usually work on a billing period, which can vary. Common billing periods are weekly or monthly. The invoice reflects all loan signings conducted during that period.

- **Payment terms:** The signing service or hiring entity reviews the LSA's invoice and processes payment based on their agreed terms. Payment may be issued via check, direct deposit, or another agreed-upon method.
- **Payment timeframe:** The time it takes to receive payment can vary depending on the signing service or hiring entity's payment schedule. LSAs should be aware of the agreed-upon payment terms and any delays that might occur.
- **Confirmation of payment:** Once payment is received, LSAs may receive a confirmation of payment along with details about the specific loan signings covered by that payment.

It's important for LSAs to maintain accurate records of their loan signings, invoices, and payment receipts. Additionally, they should establish clear payment terms and expectations with the signing services or hiring entities they work with to ensure timely and accurate compensation for their services.

The Process

Below are general step-by-step guidelines for successfully completing your first notarization or signing appointment. The process can vary slightly by state, so make sure you're aware of your state's official requirements before getting started.

Notarization Process

Step 1: Verify Identity

Ask the signer to provide identification, like a government-issued photo ID. Make sure that the ID is valid and has not expired.

Step 2: Check the Document

Confirm that the name on the ID matches the name on the document to be notarized. Verify that the document does not contain any blank spaces. Carefully review the notary certificate wording to make sure it conforms to the requirements of your state.

Step 3: Screen the Signer

Verify that the signer is willingly and knowingly signing the document. Confirm that the signer is not under duress or coercion.

Step 4: Administer the Oath or Affirmation (If Required)

If the document requires an oath or affirmation, ask the signer to recite it. The oath typically involves swearing to the truthfulness of the document's contents.

Step 5: Witness the Signature

Observe the signer as they sign the document. Ensure that the signature matches the one on the ID.

Step 6: Record in Journal

Note the notarization details in your notary journal. This is considered good practice and required by many states.

Step 7: Complete the Notarial Certificate

Fill out the notarial certificate, including the venue, the date, your notary seal or stamp, and your signature. Make sure to follow your state's specific notarial certificate requirements.

Step 8: Return the Document

Give the notarized document back to the signer. Thank them for choosing your services.

Loan Signing Process (LSAs)

Step 1: Preparation

You will receive the loan package from the hiring entity, which includes all loan documents. You will need to review the instructions to familiarize yourself with the signing requirements.

Step 2: Scheduling

Coordinate with the borrower and the hiring entity to schedule a convenient signing appointment. Confirm the appointment date, time, and location.

Step 3: Pre-Signing Review

Review the loan documents in the package to ensure they are complete and accurate. Confirm that all signatures and initials are in the correct places.

Step 4: Meeting With the Borrower

Meet the borrower at the scheduled location, typically their home or a neutral site. Present your identification and introduce yourself as the loan signing agent.

Step 5: Guiding the Signing

Guide the borrower through each document, explaining the purpose and significance of each. Ensure that signatures, initials, and dates are completed correctly. Verify the borrower's identity during the signing process. Keep in mind that you should never give legal advice.

Step 6: Notarization (If Required)

If any documents require notarization, follow the notarization process as outlined in the previous section.

Step 7: Document Organization

Organize the signed documents, place them in the provided packaging, and ensure all pages are accounted for.

Step 8: Return Documents

Promptly return the signed and organized documents to the hiring entity as instructed.

Step 9: Confirmation and Payment

Confirm with the hiring entity that the documents were received and are in order. You can expect payment based on the agreed-upon terms and billing cycle.

Please note that LSAs should also comply with their state's notarial requirements during the loan signing process, including notarizing any documents as needed. This is one of the reasons why training is so important!

Additionally, communication and professionalism are critical throughout the signing appointment to ensure a smooth and successful experience for the borrower.

Tips and Advice

As you start your exciting new career as a notary public and LSA, remember that each notarization and signing appointment is a chance to make a positive impact in the lives of others.

Here are some tips to help you make the most of this role:

- **Attention to detail:** Pay meticulous attention to the details of every document you handle. Accuracy is crucial in this profession.
- **Continuous learning:** Stay informed about updates to notary laws and loan document procedures.

Remember, education is an ongoing process as statutes and requirements can change over time.

- **Professionalism:** Present yourself with professionalism, courtesy, and integrity at all times. Your reputation is important.
- **Building your network:** Take the time to build positive relationships with clients, signing services, title companies, and borrowers. Networking can lead to repeat business.
- **Time management:** Manage your time effectively to meet appointments and deadlines. Punctuality is a hallmark of reliability.
- **Organization:** Keep your documents, records, and supplies well-organized to streamline your workflow.
- **Flexibility:** Be adaptable and willing to accommodate clients' needs within the bounds of your legal responsibilities.
- **Ethical conduct:** Always adhere to ethical standards and notarial laws. Your role as a notary is rooted in trust.
- **Customer service:** Provide excellent customer service, addressing any questions or concerns professionally.

Remember that every accomplished notary and LSA started with their first notarization or loan signing appointment. Each experience is an opportunity to learn and grow in your career. Stay committed and passionate, and your journey in this rewarding profession will lead to success.

Chapter 4

Your Professional Reputation

In this chapter, we will look at the essential principles and practices that will ensure that you maintain a sterling reputation. Whether you are a seasoned notary or just starting out, the insights and guidance here will help you safeguard your standing, build trust with clients, and uphold the highest standards of integrity throughout your career.

The Importance of a Professional Reputation

A professional reputation as a notary public and LSA means being well-regarded for your work by both your clients and your peers. This requires staying up-to-date on your commission and certification, as well as investing in ongoing education.

Maintaining a professional reputation as a notary public and loan signing agent will positively impact your business in a number of ways.

Trust and Credibility

A notary public is entrusted with verifying the authenticity of important documents and ensuring the legality of transactions. Your reputation as a trustworthy professional helps build credibility with clients, signers, and the community at large.

Legal Compliance

Notaries are subject to specific state and federal laws and regulations governing their conduct and responsibilities. Maintaining a professional reputation means that you abide by these legal requirements, avoid ethical violations, and, in doing so, prevent legal consequences.

Continued Business

Clients, including signing services, title companies, and individuals, are more likely to work with notaries and LSAs who have a proven track record of reliability and professionalism. This can lead to repeat business and referrals.

Career Advancement

A strong professional track record opens doors to opportunities for career advancement within the notary and loan signing industry. It may lead to more lucrative assignments, partnerships, or even the ability to train and mentor others.

Prioritizing professionalism in your role as a notary public and LSA is a commitment to ethical conduct, legal compliance, and the well-being of the community you serve. It creates a foundation for trust and reliability that is necessary for a successful career.

The Renewal Process

A key part of maintaining your reputation in the industry is keeping an up-to-date commission and certification at all times.

While the renewal process for notary publics in the US varies by state, below are some common steps that apply in most cases.

Renewal Eligibility

Notaries must first determine whether or not they are qualified for renewal. Eligibility requirements may include possessing an active notary commission, not having committed any severe legal or ethical offenses, and satisfying any continuing education requirements.

Notification of Renewal

Many states send renewal notices to notaries a few months before their existing commission expires. These notices may include instructions and renewal deadlines.

Renewal Application

Notaries must typically complete a renewal application issued by their state's notary commissioning body. The application may be offered either online or on paper.

Payment or Renewal Fee

A renewal fee is normally required in order for the renewal application to be processed. The charge varies by state and may also be determined by the period of the renewed commission (for example, four or six years).

Continuing Education (If Required)

As part of the renewal process, several states require notaries to complete a certain number of hours of continuing education. Notaries must finish and present proof of completion for the appropriate courses.

Background Check and Fingerprinting (If Required)

As part of the renewal procedure, some states may require notaries to undergo a background check and fingerprinting. This criteria must be met in order to renew.

Renewal Submission

Notaries must submit their renewal application, fees, and other necessary documentation (such as proof of ongoing education or background checks) to the proper notary commissioning body. Depending on the state, this can be done online, via mail, or in person.

Review and Processing

The renewal application and documentation are reviewed by the notary commissioning authority to confirm that all requirements have been met. This may include checking the notary's eligibility and the findings of the background check.

Renewal Certificate

Once the renewal application is approved, the notary will receive a new commission certificate or card, which will include the effective date and expiration date of the renewed commission.

Recordkeeping

Notaries should keep a copy of their renewal documents, including the renewal certificate, in their notary journal for record-keeping.

Notary Stamp or Seal Update (If Applicable)

If the notary is required to use a physical stamp or seal, they must ensure that it matches the revised commission dates and information.

It is essential for notaries to renew before their current commission expires to avoid a gap in their notarial authority. Failure to renew on time may require the notary to reapply as a new notary public and meet the initial application requirements.

The National Notary Association recommends that you consider the renewal process at least six months prior to the expiration date listed on your commission. When doing so, it's important to consult your specific state's notary commissioning authority or official website for the most up-to-date information, as renewal requirements can change.

In terms of the renewal process for LSAs, the Signing Professionals Workgroup recommends that LSAs renew their exam and background check every year.

Ongoing Education

Continuing education and training are essential for notaries and LSAs to stay updated with industry trends, changes in laws, and best practices.

Here are some recommendations for ongoing education and training:

- **Attend workshops and seminars:** Look for local workshops or seminars that focus on notarial practices, legal updates, and industry developments. These events provide valuable insights and networking opportunities.
- **Online courses:** Many organizations offer online courses and webinars specifically designed for notaries or LSAs. These courses can be completed and accessed at your own pace.
- **Join notary associations:** You may want to join a notary association or organization in your state or nationally. These associations often provide access to educational resources, newsletters, and events.

- **Legal updates:** Stay informed about changes in notary laws and regulations in your state. Check your state's notary commissioning authority website for updates and subscribe to relevant newsletters or mailing lists.
- **Advanced training:** If you are interested in specializing in certain areas, such as loan document signings or immigration forms, you may need additional training and certification in the specific field of your choice.
- **Professional journals:** Subscribe to professional journals or magazines that cover notarial practices and legal updates. These publications can help you stay informed.
- **Networking:** Make it a priority to meet and network with other notaries or LSAs in your area or online communities. Networking can provide valuable insights and opportunities to learn from other's experiences.
- **Review best practices:** Regularly review best practices for notarial acts and document handling. Following these guidelines will ensure the highest ethical and professional standards.
- **Mentorship:** Seek mentorship from experienced notaries or industry professionals. Learning from someone with more experience can be incredibly valuable.
- **Attend conferences:** If possible, attend notary or LSA conferences, conventions, or industry expos. These events often feature educational sessions and opportunities to interact with industry experts.
- **Read industry books:** Invest in books that cover notarial practices, legal requirements, and document handling. This can give you a deeper insight and keep you updated with current requirements.

Remember that ongoing education is not just about compliance; it's also about improving your skills and staying at the forefront of your profession. It's an investment in your career as a notary public and LSA, ensuring that you can provide the best service to your clients and the community.

Part Two

Start and Promote Your Business

Chapter 5

Getting Your First Client in 24 Hours

You've worked hard to obtain your notary commission, complete your LSA certification, and learn the ropes of your new profession. At last, it's time to put your credentials to use and earn your first income by landing your very first clients!

We understand that taking the first step into your new business venture can be both thrilling and terrifying, but we are here to help you every step of the way. Our simple, three-step system is designed to provide you with the exact strategies needed to secure your initial clients quickly and easily.

By following our advice, you will be on your way to kick-starting your business and experiencing the satisfaction of turning your passion into profit. Let's dive in and make your first 24 hours in the industry a smashing success!

Step 1: Spread the Word

Tell Everyone. Yes, Everyone.

The power of word-of-mouth cannot be overstated. Start by spreading the word among your immediate circle—your friends, coworkers, and regular contacts. Mention your new notarial and LSA services at gatherings, dinners, and conversations. You will be amazed at how many people within your existing network may require notary services or know someone who does.

Think beyond your inner circle, too. Strike up conversations with people at your yoga class, your kids' soccer games, or your local community events. Casual discussions often lead to opportunities, and you will find that many people are searching for reliable notary services for their personal and business needs.

Engage With Local Businesses

Your community is filled with businesses that regularly require notarial or LSA services. Real estate agents, law firms, mortgage lenders, healthcare providers, government agencies, employment agencies, and small businesses all have a recurring need for notarizations or loan signings.

Approach these businesses with confidence and explain how your services can benefit them:

- **Real estate agents:** Let them know you can efficiently handle loan signings and document notarizations, ensuring a smooth closing process for their clients.
- **Law firms:** Emphasize your attention to detail in notarizing legal documents and your role in maintaining the integrity of important agreements.
- **Healthcare providers:** Stress the importance of proper documentation in healthcare and how your services can assist with consent forms and medical directives.

- **Government agencies:** Highlight your commitment to accuracy and ethics when notarizing government-related documents.
- **Employment agencies:** Discuss the convenience of on-site notarizations for employee paperwork and contracts.
- **Small businesses:** Explain how your services can streamline their paperwork processes, saving time and effort.

By proactively engaging with these businesses and showcasing the value you bring as a notary and LSA, you open the door to potential partnerships and referrals.

Remember, every interaction is an opportunity. Approach Step 1 with enthusiasm and confidence in the value you offer. Building a profitable client base starts with the connections you make, and each conversation brings you one step closer to your first successful notarization or loan signing. You've got this!

Step 2: Offer Discounts

As you spread the word about your notary and LSA services, you should offer potential clients an irresistible incentive—a 50% discount! This isn't just any discount; it's your "grand opening" special, available for one day only.

Here's how to use this strategy to gain instant clients for your budding business:

Encourage First-Time Clients

A 50% discount is a powerful motivator. It entices individuals and businesses to take a chance on your services.

Even those with established notary or LSA relationships might be intrigued by the prospect of saving 50% on their usual fees. This special offer can tempt them to explore your services, perhaps for noncritical documents or as a backup option.

By offering this limited-time deal, you're removing potential barriers and making it an easy decision for first-time clients to give you a try.

Create Urgency and Excitement

Emphasize that this discount is available for 24 hours only. This sense of urgency compels potential clients to act swiftly, resulting in immediate business for you. People are more likely to commit when they're getting an exclusive deal.

Showcase Your Value

While the discount is the hook, don't forget to communicate the value you bring as a notary and LSA. Highlight your professionalism, attention to detail, and commitment to accuracy. Explain how your services can simplify their notarization or loan signing process.

Promote Your Grand Opening Special

Use social media platforms to announce your new business and share discount details. Create eye-catching flyers or digital banners to spread the word in your community or online.

Leverage your existing network, including family, friends, and business contacts, to help you promote the special offer. Just keep in mind that while family can help you spread the word about your business, they generally can't be your clients, as this presents a conflict of interest.

Remember, Step 2 isn't just about the discount; it's about seizing the opportunity to showcase your skills and professionalism to a wider audience. Once clients experience the quality of your service, they may become loyal regulars for years to come.

So, set a date for your "grand opening," prepare to impress, and get ready to welcome your first wave of satisfied clients!

Step 3: Ask for a Testimonial

Congratulations on securing your first clients through the "grand opening" special! Now, let's take the success a step further by harnessing the power of testimonials.

Here's how asking for testimonials can bolster your reputation and drive future business:

- **Leverage Satisfied Clients:** Your clients are already thrilled with the discount they received, and if they are pleased with your services, they are likely to be happy to provide a testimonial. Their positive experiences can be your most compelling marketing tool.
- **Build Credibility:** Testimonials from real clients offer an authentic and trustworthy perspective on your services. They build credibility by showcasing your ability to meet and exceed expectations.
- **Ease Potential Clients' Concerns:** Prospective clients often have reservations when trying a new service. Testimonials from satisfied clients provide reassurance and answer questions they may have about your professionalism and competence.

How to Request Testimonials

Reach out to clients with a personalized message expressing your gratitude for their business. Let them know that their feedback would be invaluable in helping your new venture.

Make it easy for clients to provide testimonials by offering clear instructions. Ask them to write one or two sentences about their experience with your services. Make sure that clients are comfortable with their testimonials being used on your website or marketing materials. Respect their privacy and confidentiality.

As you receive testimonials, showcase them proudly on your website and in your marketing materials. This not only reinforces your credibility but also encourages more clients to share their positive experiences.

Instead of (or in addition to) a testimonial, you can ask clients to review your business on Google, Yelp, or Facebook. You can also request that they refer your services to their family or friends. This encourages a positive feedback loop that will bring new clients right to your door!

We understand that reaching out for testimonials can be intimidating, but remember, your clients are your biggest advocates. Offer them words of encouragement and gratitude for considering your request. Let them know how much their feedback means to your growing business.

By taking these simple steps, you are not only creating buzz about your new venture but also setting the stage for future success. Each satisfied client and glowing testimonial propels you further on your journey as a notary public and loan signing agent. So, go ahead, ask for those testimonials, and watch your business thrive.

As you conclude this chapter, take a moment to look back at how far you've come. You've spread the word, offered compelling discounts, and gathered valuable testimonials; each action takes you closer to your dreams of success as a notary public and loan signing agent.

Remember, every client you serve and every testimonial you collect are building blocks in the foundation of your thriving business. It may seem daunting to build your business at times, but with each step forward, you are making your dreams a reality.

In the chapters that follow, you will find valuable insights, strategies, and guidance to ensure your business runs smoothly and continues to flourish. So, stay committed, stay motivated, and believe in yourself, for you are well on your way to achieving your dreams.

Chapter 6

Six-Figure Marketing

Doing business without advertising is like winking at a girl in the dark. You know what you are doing, but nobody else does. –Steuart Henderson Britt

Now that you've secured your first clients, let's look at strategies to catapult your business to new heights. This is where the magic happens—in the world of marketing.

Let's begin by addressing a fundamental truth: a thriving notarial and loan signing business relies on effective marketing. You could be the most skilled notary or LSA in your region, but if no one knows about your services, your skills remain underutilized. Marketing is the vehicle that propels your business into the spotlight, connecting you with potential clients who are actively seeking notarial or signing services.

In the increasingly competitive landscape of notarial services, a robust marketing strategy is your secret to success. It's the difference between maintaining a modest clientele and transforming your business into a lucrative six-figure enterprise.

In today's digital age, the internet is the linchpin of marketing success. Most individuals and businesses in need of local notarial or signing services turn to online platforms to find what they seek.

This chapter will equip you with the knowledge and tools to leverage the online sphere and reach a broader audience than ever before. Online marketing tactics range from developing a professional website to improving your online presence through search engines and social media. It is a dynamic environment that allows you to interact with potential customers, build trust, and establish your authority in the notarial field.

While online marketing is powerful on its own, we believe in a more thorough approach. Your marketing toolkit should go beyond the digital world. This chapter will look at a variety of both online and offline marketing tactics. The combination of these tactics will launch your business to six-figure success.

While we'll explore various marketing strategies in this chapter, feel free to choose as many or as few as you'd like for your business. If you're only working on your notarial venture a few hours per week, you can build a significant client base with just the basics, such as a website, social media, and notary directories. If you're looking to expand your client base even further, you can also leverage blogging, email marketing, and so much more. The choice is yours.

Before we dive in, please note that states may have specific restrictions or guidelines related to advertising to ensure that notaries don't misrepresent their role or services. Be sure to do any research that is relevant to your state before getting started.

The world of notarial services is full of opportunities, and it's up to you to seize them. The principles you will learn in this chapter are tried-and-true techniques that have propelled countless notaries and LSAs to the pinnacles of their careers. The journey to six figures begins with a compelling marketing strategy, and we are here to guide you every step of the way.

Online Marketing Strategies

All six-figure businesses have a strong online presence; the goal is to have your business appear front and center when potential clients are searching for the services you provide.

Website

Having a website is increasingly important for any business for several compelling reasons:

- **Professional image:** A well-designed website conveys professionalism and competence. It's often the first impression a potential client has of your business. A professional website instills trust and confidence in your services.
- **Information hub:** Your website serves as a central hub for information about your services. Clients can access details about your offerings, pricing, contact information, and business hours, making it a convenient resource for them.
- **Marketing and promotion:** Your website is a powerful tool for marketing and promotion. You can use it to showcase client testimonials, highlight your expertise, and explain the benefits of your services. It is an excellent platform for persuading potential clients to choose you.

In sum, setting up a website is a vital step for establishing your online presence.

Here's a general overview of the process, along with some recommendations:

- **Domain name and hosting:** A domain name is the web address that users will type into their browsers to access your website. For example, "YourNameNotary.com". Hosting is where your website's files and data are stored, making them accessible to visitors on the internet. We recommend looking at Bluehost or SiteGround, as they're reliable and cost-effective hosting providers.

- **Choosing a domain name:** Your domain name should ideally be your name or your business name, as this makes it easy for people to remember and find you online. You can check the availability of your chosen domain name by visiting sites like Namecheap.com. If your preferred domain name is available, you can register it for your website.

- **Creating your website:** You can build your website through builders like WordPress, Wix, or Squarespace. These platforms offer user-friendly interfaces, templates, and customization options. Install the chosen website builder through your hosting provider. Wix and Squarespace come with hosting, while WordPress requires a separate hosting provider. Installation is typically easy and hosting companies often offer one-click installations.

- **Website design:** Your website's design should be clean, user-friendly, and mobile-responsive. Many visitors access websites on their smartphones, so make sure your website looks good on mobile devices.

- **Promotion:** Once your website is live, promote it through your business cards, social media, and other marketing materials. Encourage satisfied clients to visit and provide testimonials.

Minimum website content:

Make sure your website includes essential information like

- your name and contact information, including a contact form for inquiries.
- a list of the services you offer, clearly explained.
- the hours that you're available for notarization or loan signing services.
- information about the geographic area you serve and how far you're willing to travel.

Optional (but highly recommended) website content:

For a more informative and engaging website, consider adding

- a professional photo of yourself along with a section detailing your background, training, and experience. This helps potential clients get to know you.
- testimonials from previous clients. Positive feedback builds trust and reassures potential clients.
- links to your social media profiles. Social media can be used to further engage with your clients and to market your business.
- a pop up form so those who are interested can sign up for your email list.
- a blog section where you can regularly post articles related to notarial and loan signing topics. This can establish you as an authority in your field and improve your website's search engine ranking.

Setting up a website might seem like a daunting task, but with the right hosting provider and website builder, it can be a relatively straightforward process. Your website is a powerful tool to showcase your services, engage with clients, and grow your notarial and loan signing business.

SEO

Search engine optimization (SEO) is a powerful tool that can significantly enhance your online presence as a notary public and loan signing agent. By understanding and implementing the fundamentals of SEO, your business can appear on the first page of search engine results when potential clients are searching for the services you offer.

Here's what you need to know:

Why SEO Matters

When potential clients are in need of notarial or loan signing services, their first action is often to turn to search engines like Google. Appearing on the first page of search results is crucial because most users rarely venture beyond this page. SEO techniques help your website rank higher in search results, making it more likely that potential clients will find and choose your services.

Keyword Research

SEO is all about keywords. Keywords are the terms or phrases that people type into search engines when looking for specific information or services. For example, someone might search for "notary services in Ohio."

To optimize SEO effectively, you should do the following:

- **Perform keyword research:** This involves identifying the keywords that potential clients are most likely to use when searching for services like yours. Various online tools can assist with this research, such as Google Keyword Planner and Google Trends, helping you determine which keywords are most relevant to your business.
- **Utilize long-tail keywords:** Long-tail keywords are longer, more specific keyword phrases typically composed of three to five words. They are highly valuable because they target users who are closer to making a decision or a purchase. For instance, instead of simply using "notary service" as a keyword, you might optimize your website for "notarize a car title in Ohio." This more specific keyword is more likely to attract potential clients who are in need of your exact services.

Where to Use Keywords

To maximize the impact of your chosen keywords, you should strategically incorporate them into your website. Consider the following:

- **Title tags.** Include relevant keywords in the title tags of your web pages. These tags provide a concise description of the content on the page and are visible in search results.
- **Headers and content.** Use keywords naturally in the headers and content of your website. However, avoid overusing them, as this can negatively impact your site's ranking.
- **Meta descriptions.** Write informative meta descriptions for your web pages that contain relevant

keywords. Meta descriptions are the brief snippets that appear in search results below the title.

- **Image alt text.** If you include images on your website, use keyword-rich alt text for them. This is not only useful for SEO but also makes your site more accessible for users with visual impairments. Just make sure that the keywords you're using accurately describe the image. Be careful not to "keyword stuff" by adding too many.
- **URLs.** Craft descriptive URLs that include relevant keywords. This not only helps with SEO but also makes it easier for users to understand the content of your web pages.

More SEO tips for better results include the following:

- **Create high-quality content.** The content on your website should be valuable, relevant, and well-written. Informative and engaging content not only attracts visitors but also keeps them on your site longer. This reduces your bounce rate, or the percentage of users that leave your website after viewing only one page, which can have a positive impact on your ranking.
- **Mobile optimization.** Ensure that your website is mobile-friendly. Google gives preference to mobile-optimized sites as an increasing number of users access the web on mobile devices.
- **Optimize page speed.** A slow website can result in higher bounce rates. Speed up your site by optimizing images, leveraging browser caching, and using a content delivery network (CDN).
- **Secure your website.** Implement HTTPS to ensure a secure connection. This not only protects user data but is also a ranking factor in Google's algorithms.

- **Local SEO.** If you serve a specific geographic area, optimize your website for local search by including your location in key places, such as in your content and meta descriptions.
- **Use header tags.** Use header tags (H1, H2, H3, etc.) to structure your content. These tags help search engines understand the hierarchy of your content.
- **Internal linking.** Link to reputable external sources when they add value to your content. This can enhance your credibility and relevance.
- **Regular update.** Keep your website updated with fresh content. Regularly publishing new blog posts or articles can help with SEO, as it demonstrates that your site is active and informative.
- **User experience.** Ensure your website provides an excellent user experience. A user-friendly design, easy navigation, and clear calls to action can improve user engagement.
- **Optimize images.** Compress images to reduce file sizes and use descriptive file names and alt text to improve accessibility and SEO.
- **Monitor analytics.** Use tools like Google Analytics to track your website's performance. Regularly review your data to identify what is working and what needs improvement.
- **Social media integration.** Promote your website through social media channels. Social signals can indirectly impact your SEO by increasing your online presence.

It takes time to see SEO results, so be patient and consistently apply these tips to enhance your online visibility and attract more clients to your notarial and loan signing business.

Google Business Profile

Google Business Profile, formerly known as Google My Business, is a free tool that Google offers to help businesses and organizations manage their online presence on Google's search engine and Google Maps. This tool is crucial for local business owners, including notary publics and loan signing agents, as it helps potential clients find, connect with, and learn more about your business.

You can provide essential information about your business, including your name, address, phone number, and website. This information is displayed prominently in Google search results and on Google Maps, making it easier for potential clients to find and contact you. You can also set up your business hours to inform potential clients when you are available for notarizations or loan signings.

The platform allows you to upload images and videos that showcase your work, office, or team. You can also create posts about news, updates, events, or special offers related to your business. These posts can also appear in search results and on Maps, keeping potential clients informed and engaged.

Clients can also rate and review your business on the platform. Positive reviews can boost your credibility and attract more clients, while negative reviews give you the opportunity to address concerns and improve your services.

Another valuable tool is Google Insights. This tool provides valuable data on how often your profile is viewed and how clients discover your business. Insights helps you understand your online performance, and you can adjust your strategy accordingly.

A well-maintained Google Business Profile is an essential part of your online marketing strategy, particularly for local services like your business. It helps potential clients find you easily, learn about your business, and contact you with inquiries or appointment requests. By keeping your profile up-to-date and engaging with clients, you can effectively enhance your online presence and attract more business.

Blogging

Blogging can be another powerful tool in promoting your notary and loan signing business. It offers a number of unique benefits that can help you grow your online presence and attract more clients.

Blogging allows you to demonstrate your expertise in the fields of notarial and loan signing services, while also keeping your website fresh and engaging. When you provide valuable information and insights, you establish yourself as an authority in your industry. This can instill trust and confidence in potential clients.

Your blog posts should educate clients and the public through sharing information that relates to notarial services, loan signings, and related topics. For instance, you can write about the process for notarizing specific documents, steps to prevent identity theft, or explain which documents require notarization in your state.

When choosing topics for blog posts, you should perform keyword research to determine the information that your potential clients are searching for. Clients who find value in your blog are more likely to refer to your services and to share your content with others.

Blogging can also be an effective SEO tool. When you create blog posts with relevant keywords, you increase the likelihood of your content appearing on the first page of search engine results. For example, if you write a post on "notary services in Ohio," optimizing your content can help potential clients in your state find your business.

In this way, blogging can also serve as a marketing platform. You can promote your services, special offers, and events through your blog posts. This helps you reach a wider audience and can lead to more inquiries and bookings.

By consistently producing high-quality, relevant content, you can build trust, attract more clients, and contribute to the growth of your business.

Social Media

Social media is a dynamic and highly effective tool for promoting your business. It offers a range of benefits, from connecting with potential clients to building your brand and showcasing your expertise.

To maximize the impact of your social media efforts, start by researching the two platforms where your potential clients are most likely to spend their time. Focusing your efforts on these channels ensures that you are reaching your target audience effectively.

LinkedIn

LinkedIn is a professional networking platform. It's an excellent choice for notary publics and LSAs, as it allows you to connect with other professionals and businesses in your industry.

Tips for using LinkedIn effectively include

- creating a professional LinkedIn profile that highlights your experience and expertise.
- joining in discussions to expand your network and share valuable insights.
- leveraging relevant hashtags to increase visibility and using mentions to boost engagement.

Facebook

With its huge user base, Facebook is a versatile platform for building your brand and engaging with potential clients. You can create a business page to showcase your services.

Tips for using Facebook effectively include

- regularly posting content that informs and educates your audience about notarial services.
- using images and videos to make your posts more engaging.
- encouraging client reviews and responding to inquiries promptly.

X (Formerly Known as Twitter)

X is great for sharing short, concise updates and engaging with your audience in real time. It is particularly effective for announcing events or sharing industry news.

Tips for using X effectively include

- sharing quick tips and links to your blog posts, and engaging in conversations with industry peers and potential clients.
- using relevant hashtags in posts to reach a broader audience.
- using the search feature to find potential clients by searching for hashtags or keywords that are relevant to your services.

YouTube

While not a traditional social media platform, YouTube is a valuable channel for sharing informative videos about notarial or loan signing topics. Videos can be a powerful way to showcase your expertise.

Tips for using YouTube effectively include

- creating short, informative videos about the notarization process, answering common client questions, or explaining various documents.
- embedding your videos on your website, so it's easy for clients to find and engage with them.
- optimizing video titles and descriptions for SEO to reach a wider audience.

Pinterest

Pinterest is ideal for businesses with a blog. You can use it to promote your blog posts through visually appealing pins. It's especially effective for sharing information-rich content.

Tips for using Pinterest effectively include

- designing eye-catching pins with informative visuals.
- creating boards related to different aspects of notarial services.
- engaging with other pinners by "repinning" and commenting on their content.
- using a pin scheduler, such as Tailwind, to post at regular intervals throughout the day.

To succeed on social media, the secret is to be consistent. Show up on your chosen platforms every day or at the frequency that suits your schedule. Consistency builds trust and keeps your audience engaged.

By using the right social media channels and regularly engaging with your audience, you can create a strong online presence for your notarial and loan signing business. Social media is an excellent platform for building your brand, sharing knowledge, and connecting with potential clients, ultimately leading to business growth.

Email Marketing

Client retention is a cornerstone of success in the notary and loan signing industries. Your clients are the lifeblood of your business, and staying in touch with them is vital. One effective way to achieve this is through email marketing.

For any business, but especially in the notary and loan signing business, building lasting relationships with clients is crucial. Client retention means repeat business and referrals, and email marketing can be a powerful tool to maintain these relationships and keep your business top-of-mind. A great way to do this is to send out a regular email newsletter.

Email Newsletter

We recommend sending a monthly email newsletter to your clients. This regular communication helps you stay at the forefront of their minds and demonstrates your commitment to providing value beyond your services.

Your email newsletter can include a variety of content, such as the following:

- **Updates about your business.** Share news, recent accomplishments, or upcoming events related to your notarial services.

- **Personal touch.** Add a personal touch by including anecdotes or family photos. Let your clients get to know you as a person, not just as a service provider.
- **Inspirational quote or fun fact.** These can add a positive and engaging element to your newsletter.
- **Educational tips.** Offer valuable information, such as tips on preventing identity theft or explaining the various documents that may require your services.
- **Express gratitude.** Thank your subscribers for being a part of your email list. Remind them of your business hours and the range of services you offer. Some clients may not realize the full scope of your offerings.

Selecting an Email Marketing Platform

To send emails to your subscribers, you will need an email marketing platform. Some options you may want to consider are below:

- **ConvertKit:** A user-friendly platform often preferred by content creators.
- **Mailchimp:** Known for its simplicity and a free plan that is great for beginners.
- **Constant Contact:** Offers a range of features for small businesses, including email marketing.

Collecting Email Addresses

To build your email list, use your email marketing platform to add a popup form to your website. This allows you to collect email addresses easily.

You can also encourage clients to subscribe by promoting your newsletter through your social media channels and in your physical office space.

Tips for Your Email Marketing Strategy

- **Use a catchy subject line.** There is no use in sending an email with great content if the subject line is not compelling. You can even consider including emojis to lighten the mood and use power words to get a response from your readers.
- **Share thought-provoking articles.** Instead of trying to sell your services directly, you can share your expertise by linking to a relevant piece you wrote for your blog.
- **Use A/B testing for your marketing campaigns.** Split testing is a great way to try several advertising strategies and see which ones work best with your audience. In this way, you can experiment with a new strategy before fully committing. Some email marketing platforms even have A/B testing tools built into their features. For example, with ConvertKit, you can split test two different subject lines to see which one results in a higher open rate.
- **Optimize your sending time.** You will need to do some research in your community about when people typically access their emails. It is no use, for example, to send emails over the weekends, but you may find Tuesday mornings to be better.
- **Send targeted email campaigns.** Don't spam your audience with emails, but make sure each email makes an impact. Stick to your monthly newsletter unless there are

important issues that your audience needs to take note of, for example, changes in legal requirements.

- **Personalize it.** Include their name or nickname in the subject line, talk about the things they have expressed interest in, and offer birthday greetings and special offerings.

Paid Advertising

Paid advertising is a potent tool that can significantly enhance the visibility of your business in search results. It is particularly useful when you want your listings to appear prominently for specific keywords or in competitive markets.

While it is not always a necessity, it can be highly effective in the right circumstances. We recommend Facebook ads (technically known as "Meta ads") and Google Ads, as they typically have the best results.

Facebook Ads

Facebook ads allow you to create targeted ads that appear on Facebook and Instagram. These ads can be tailored to reach specific demographics and interests. To get the best results, you may want to consider the following:

- **Audience targeting.** Use Facebook's advanced targeting options to reach the right audience, like individuals in your local area or those interested in notarial services.
- **Compelling ad content.** Create ad content that is informative, engaging, and includes a call to action, like visiting your website or contacting your business.

- **Training.** Make use of the many articles, books, and free courses available to improve results from your Facebook ads.

Google Ads

Google Ads are pay-per-click (PPC) ads that appear in Google search results. You bid on specific keywords, and your ad is displayed when users search for those keywords. To succeed with Google Ads, follow these strategies:

- **Keyword research.** Conduct thorough keyword research to identify the terms your potential clients are searching for. This helps you target the most relevant keywords.
- **Compelling ad content**: Write ad copy that directly addresses the needs of your clients and encourages them to click on your ad.
- **Quality score.** Improve your quality score by ensuring that your ad and landing page are relevant to the keywords you are targeting.

While paid advertising can be highly effective, it's important to consider your budget. Paid advertising, especially on Google Ads, can become costly if not managed effectively. It's often best used in conjunction with other strategies, like SEO.

Notary Directories

Notary directories are a valuable resource that can significantly boost your business. They serve as platforms that provide a list of reliable notaries, making it easier for individuals and businesses to find your services.

Notary directories offer both free and paid listing options. While some directories allow you to list your business for free, others may charge a fee for enhanced visibility or additional features. You may want to consider having a paid listing in at least one directory, as it can provide more exposure that will help you stand out from the competition.

Being listed in reputable notary directories helps legitimize your business. Potential clients often turn to these platforms when seeking notarial services. Your presence on such directories enhances your credibility and trustworthiness in their eyes.

To make the most of your listing, provide as much information as possible. Beyond your name and email address, include details like your contact number, business address, a brief bio, your service areas, and any relevant certifications or credentials. High-quality photos and a professional profile description can also make your listing more appealing to potential clients.

Recommended Online Notary Directories

There are several notary directories to consider, but here are a few recommendations:

- **123Notary:** A respected and widely recognized directory that connects notaries with clients.
- **Notary Rotary:** Known for its comprehensive listings and user-friendly interface.
- **Notary Café:** A platform that focuses on connecting notaries with potential clients and allows for extensive profile customization.
- **SigningAgent.com:** Run by the National Notary Association (NNA), this directory is highly regarded. If you have purchased one of the NNA's loan signing agent

certification packages, you may receive a one-year listing on SigningAgent.com for free.

Other Marketing Strategies

To achieve a thriving business and reach your income goals, it's essential to embrace a multifaceted marketing approach. Beyond digital and online strategies, here are some other strategies you may want to consider.

Word-of-Mouth Marketing

Continue to inform your friends and social circles about your notarial services. Word-of-mouth referrals can be incredibly effective. You can also request that satisfied clients recommend your services.

Promotional Merchandise

Consider creating promotional items like pens featuring your business name and logo. Distribute these to local businesses that could refer clients to you, like insurance agents, financial advisors, or real estate agents.

Community Involvement

Engage with your local community by attending events, fairs, or meetings. Becoming a visible and supportive member of your community can build trust and connections that lead to referrals.

Social Responsibility

Offer free or discounted notarizations to local nonprofit organizations, schools, teachers, nurses, or military personnel. This generous gesture not only supports your community but also generates positive word-of-mouth for your business.

Traditional Marketing Collateral

Use traditional marketing materials like flyers and business cards. Hand these out to potential clients and leave them at local businesses or community centers.

Local Advertising

Consider placing ads in local publications, on community websites, or even in businesses where potential clients frequently visit.

Branded Merchandise

Invest in promotional materials like T-shirts, bumper stickers, and yard signs featuring your business name and contact information. Large car signs can be very effective, turning your car into a mobile advertisement.

Responsive Communication

Ensure you have a dedicated phone number for your notary business and answer calls promptly. While digital communication is essential, offering a direct line allows clients to connect with you personally and ask questions, which helps to build trust. Most people still want the human touch when doing business.

By diversifying your marketing efforts and adopting these additional strategies, you can expand your reach and create multiple ways for clients to discover your services. Remember, it's about more than just being an excellent notary; it's about making your business known and accessible to those who need your services.

Chapter 7

Should You Form an LLC?

Congratulations on taking those initial steps in your journey as a notary public and loan signing agent. You've secured your first clients and initiated your marketing efforts, and now it's time to think about the structure of the business you are creating. Your choice in this matter can have profound implications for your business's operations, tax responsibilities, and legal obligations.

In this chapter, we'll share information about limited liability companies (LLCs) and help you understand whether forming an LLC is a suitable choice for your business. But before we get started, it's important to clarify the following:

- We will guide you through the process of establishing your business entity, from choosing a business name to registering it with the appropriate authorities.
- We are not here to complicate things; we aim to simplify the concept of LLCs and provide you with straightforward guidance. We will break down the essentials so that you can make informed decisions.

- We must acknowledge that we are not legal experts, attorneys, or professionals giving legal advice. This chapter is designed to offer general advice and insights. Your business is unique, and we strongly recommend consulting with a legal professional if you have specific concerns or need personalized guidance.

With these considerations in mind, let's begin our exploration of LLCs and whether they could benefit your business.

What is an LLC?

A limited liability company, or LLC, is a popular and adaptable corporate structure in the United States. It combines the simplicity and tax benefits of a sole proprietorship or general partnership with the liability protection of a corporation.

Here are the key aspects of an LLC:

Limited Liability

A primary advantage of an LLC is limited liability. This means that your personal assets, like your home and savings, are generally protected from the debts and legal responsibilities of your company. This implies that if your business faces financial or legal difficulties, your personal assets are typically secure from legal claims.

Pass-Through Taxation

An LLC is not taxed as a separate entity; its income is distributed to the owners (members), who record their portion of the company's profits and losses on their personal tax returns. This pass-through form simplifies taxation and potentially results in tax savings.

Flexibility

LLCs create managerial and operational flexibility. You can structure your LLC as a single-member or multimember LLC. You can also decide how revenues and losses are distributed among members, providing a flexible approach to ownership.

Simplicity of Formation

Forming an LLC is often as simple as filing articles of organization with your state's designated department. Compared to other corporate arrangements, the associated paperwork and continuing compliance needs are often less difficult.

Credibility

Forming an LLC can provide a professional and credible layer to your organization. This is especially useful when working with clients who prefer or demand notarial services from an established business.

Independent Legal Entity

While an LLC provides personal liability protection, keeping your personal and corporate finances and operations separate is critical. This ensures that your LLC's legal protection is preserved.

Receiving an EIN

Forming an LLC allows you to obtain an Employer Identification Number (EIN) from the IRS. An EIN is essential for various business-related activities, including opening a business bank account, filing taxes, and hiring employees.

Enhanced Privacy

LLCs can provide privacy by allowing you to keep your personal information separate from your business records.

Simplified Reporting

LLCs generally have less complex reporting and recordkeeping requirements than corporations, making them a practical choice for small businesses.

Managing and Regulation

LLCs can be handled in a variety of ways. They are subject to control by their members or by appointing a manager to oversee daily operations. This option allows you to structure management to meet your company's needs.

In sum, an LLC can be a great option for small business owners who want to preserve their personal assets while simplifying their operations' administrative and tax elements. But whether or not an LLC is the best option for your company is determined by various criteria, including your individual aims and circumstances.

General Costs of an LLC

The costs associated with forming and maintaining an LLC can vary depending on the state in which you operate and the specific requirements of your business.

Below, we've listed some general costs you might encounter when establishing and maintaining an LLC:

Filing Fees

Most states require the payment of filing fees when submitting the articles of organization (or equivalent documents) to register your LLC. These fees can range from $50 to $500 or more, depending on your state.

Name Reservation Fees

If you want to reserve your LLC's name before filing the articles of organization, some states may charge a separate fee for this service.

Registered Agent Fees

You may designate a registered agent for your LLC to receive legal documents and official notices on your behalf. Registered agent services can cost anywhere from $50 to $300 annually.

Annual Report Fees

Many states require LLCs to file annual reports or statements, which may involve additional fees. These fees usually range from $10 to $100 or more.

Publication Costs

In some states, LLCs are required to publish a notice in local newspapers to announce their formation. Publication costs vary widely by location.

Operating Agreements Costs

While not a state requirement, creating an operating agreement for an LLC is advisable. You may incur legal fees for drafting this document unless you create it yourself.

Business License Fees

Your local municipality may require a business license or permit, which often involves fees.

Insurance costs

Depending on your business type and location, you may need various insurance policies, such as liability insurance, which come with their own costs.

Renewal Fees

LLCs must renew their registration with the state periodically, and this renewal process may involve additional fees.

Change of Registered Agent or Business Address Fees

If you need to update your registered agent or business address, the state may charge fees for such changes.

Please note that while these costs provide a general overview, the actual expenses associated with forming and maintaining an LLC can vary considerably based on your location, the complexity of your business structure, and the services you provide. Additionally, ongoing costs, such as annual report fees, registered agent fees, and franchise taxes, will continue as long as your LLC is active.

The Process

Establishing an LLC involves several steps and varies slightly from state to state. Here is a general overview of the process:

Choose a Name

Select a unique name for your LLC that complies with your state's naming requirements. It should typically include "LLC" at the end. You should also ensure the name is not already in use by another business in your state.

Designate a Registered Agent

Appoint a registered agent who will receive legal documents and official notices on behalf of your LLC. The registered agent must have a physical address within the state of formation.

File Articles of Organization

This is a simple form you fill out and mail to the designated department within your state, along with any associated fees.

Obtain an EIN

Apply for an Employer Identification Number (EIN) from the Internal Revenue Service (IRS). An EIN is essential for tax purposes and other business-related activities.

Publish a Notice (If Required)

Some states may require LLCs to publish a notice of their formation in local newspapers. If this is necessary in your state, complete this step.

File Initial and Annual Reports

Many states require LLCs to file initial reports or statements shortly after formation and then annual reports or statements each year thereafter.

Comply With State Regulations

Familiarize yourself with your state's specific requirements for LLCs, including annual taxes, franchise taxes, and any other ongoing obligations.

Obtain Business Licenses

Depending on your location and the nature of your business, you may need local, state, or federal licenses or permits.

Open a Business Bank Account

To maintain the separation between personal and business finances, open a dedicated business bank account for your LLC. You will typically need your EIN and LLC formation documents to do this.

Throughout the process, always consult with your state's business registration agency and consider seeking legal or financial advice to ensure you're following the correct procedures for your location.

Forming an LLC can provide valuable liability protection and tax benefits, so it is worth investing the time and effort to get it right.

Business Structure

The structure of your business is important as it impacts taxation, liability, management, and more. Apart from an LLC, common organizational structures include the following:

- **Sole proprietorship:** In this structure, a single individual owns and operates the business. It's the simplest form but offers no liability protection. Profits and losses are reported on the owner's individual tax return.
- **Partnership:** A partnership involves two or more individuals co-owning and operating a business. Partners share profits, losses, and management responsibilities. There are general and limited partnerships (where some partners have limited liability).
- **C corporation:** C corporations are separate legal entities from their owners. They offer strong liability protection, but profits are taxed at the corporate level and then again when distributed to shareholders.
- **S corporation:** S corporations are business entities that have elected a special tax status with the IRS. They provide limited liability and avoid double taxation by passing profits and losses through to shareholders, who report them on their individual tax returns.
- **Limited liability partnerships (LLP):** LLPs are typically used by professionals (like lawyers and accountants) who want to maintain personal liability protection while sharing management and ownership.

- **Professional limited liability company (PLLC):** Similar to an LLC but specifically for licensed professionals, PLLCs offer liability protection to members.

Frequently Asked Questions

Should I invest in an LLC if I'm only doing this part-time?

Whether you run your business full-time or part-time, forming an LLC can be a good choice. It offers personal liability protection, which is important no matter how often you work.

Even if your business is part-time, you might have assets to protect, and an LLC can help shield your personal property from business-related debts and legal claims. Additionally, it provides a professional image and can help with marketing and client trust.

What is a "doing business as" (DBA) and when do I need one?

A "doing business as" (DBA) is a trade name or fictitious name that a business uses, often when the business's legal name is different from the name it operates under. You typically need a DBA when you want to conduct business under a name other than your own personal name or your LLC's legal name.

For example, if your LLC is named "John Smith Notary Services, LLC," but you want to use the name "Quicksign Notaries" on your business materials, you would need to register "Quicksign Notaries" as a DBA. The rules for DBA registration vary by state, so check your state's requirements to determine when you need one.

Can I form an LLC if I am the only member?

Yes, you can form a single-member LLC. It provides liability protection and allows you to report business income on your personal tax return.

Do I need an attorney to form an LLC?

It is not a legal requirement, but consulting with an attorney can ensure that your LLC is properly set up according to state laws. You can also use online formation services, such as LegalZoom, to simplify the process.

What is the difference between an LLC and a corporation?

While both offer liability protection, LLCs are typically easier to set up and have flexible management structures. Corporations can have double taxation but may offer more significant fundraising opportunities.

How do I get an EIN for my LLC?

You can obtain an Employer Identification Number (EIN) from the IRS online. It's a straightforward process that usually takes just a few minutes.

What are the benefits of an EIN?

An EIN is essential for business owners as it creates a separation between the individual and their business. You can often use your EIN instead of your Social Security Number (SSN) on business-related documents and filings.

An EIN can also help you establish a business credit history that is independent of your personal credit history. In fact, you can even secure funding for your notary public and loan signing agent business using your EIN only. This ensures your business can grow quickly without putting your personal assets at risk.

For the exact steps needed to secure trade credit, credit cards, and loans for your business using just your EIN (no SSN required), check out our book, *The Insider's Guide to Business Credit Using an EIN Only*.

How long does it take to form an LLC?

The timeline can vary by state, but it generally takes a few weeks to a few months to complete all the necessary steps to form an LLC.

Can I operate my business in multiple states with one LLC?

You can typically expand your business operations to other states, but you may need to register your LLC as a foreign entity in each state where you conduct business.

These answers should help address some of the common questions and concerns you may have when considering the formation of an LLC for your notary public and loan signing agent business. Always remember that specific rules and regulations can vary by state, so it's important to research your state's specific requirements or consult with professionals for guidance.

In the next chapter, we'll delve more deeply into taxes and insurance. We'll explore how to manage your business's financial obligations, navigate tax considerations, and protect your enterprise through insurance coverage. These critical topics are pivotal to the ongoing success and sustainability of your business.

So, let's continue our journey toward building a thriving notarial and loan signing business by addressing these important financial and risk management aspects.

Chapter 8

Taxes and Insurance

For many people, one of the most intimidating aspects of starting and running a business is the world of taxes and insurance. If you're one of those people, don't worry! We're here to help.

This chapter will unravel the complexities and uncertainties surrounding these crucial aspects of your notary public and loan signing agent business. Our mission is to make this seemingly daunting territory feel like a well-lit path, guiding you toward informed decisions and financial stability.

By breaking down these complex topics into manageable steps and providing practical guidance, we'll ensure that your notary public and loan signing agent business thrives without the worry of unforeseen tax burdens or uncovered risks.

Before we get started, just a quick reminder that we are not accountants or lawyers, and this book is not a substitute for professional financial or legal advice. It's important to consult with qualified experts, such as accountants, tax advisors, or attorneys, as they can provide tailored guidance based on your individual situation and ensure compliance with the latest regulations.

Tax Benefits

Here are some of the tax benefits you can have as a notary and LSA:

Self-Employment Tax Deduction

Self-employment taxes include Social Security and Medicare taxes for self-employed individuals. You can deduct the employer-equivalent portion of your self-employment tax when you calculate your adjusted gross income.

Tax Credits

Depending on your specific circumstances, you may qualify for certain tax credits, such as the phone and internet deduction, which allows you to claim a portion of your phone and internet-related expenses as business expenses. Be sure to research the tax credits available to your business.

Retirement Plan Contributions

Notaries and LSAs can set up retirement plans, such as simplified employee pension (SEP) IRAs or solo 401(k)s, which allow you to make tax-deductible contributions to save for retirement.

Health Insurance Premiums

If you are self-employed, you may be able to deduct the cost of health insurance premiums for yourself, your spouse, and your dependents. This deduction can reduce your taxable income.

Depreciation

For notaries and LSAs who invest in equipment or assets for their business, depreciation allows you to deduct a portion of the asset's cost over time. This reduces your taxable income, spreading the deduction over several years.

Tax Deductions

Here are some common tax deductions that notaries and loan signing agents may be eligible to claim:

Business Use of Home

If you have a dedicated workspace at home used exclusively for your notary and loan signing business, you may be able to deduct a portion of your home-related expenses, such as rent, mortgage interest, utilities, and maintenance.

Business Supplies

Deduct expenses related to office supplies, such as paper, ink, pens, stamps, notary journals, and any other materials necessary for your work.

Business Mileage

You can deduct the cost of business-related travel, such as mileage driven to client appointments, conferences, or training sessions. Keep a mileage log to track these expenses accurately.

Professional Development

Expenses incurred for notary education, training, seminars, and workshops are usually tax-deductible. This includes the cost of books, courses, and certification fees.

Professional Fees

You can typically deduct fees related to your notary commission and any professional association memberships, as these fees are considered necessary for your business.

Advertising and Marketing

Expenses for advertising your services, including business cards, website costs, and marketing materials, are often tax-deductible.

Business Insurance Premiums

Premiums for business insurance, such as E&O insurance or general liability insurance, can often be deducted.

Notary and Loan Signing Tools

Expenses related to notarization and signing tools, such as a portable printer, laptop, or tablet, may be deductible as business expenses.

Please note that tax laws can change and may vary by location, so it's often helpful to consult with a qualified tax professional to ensure you're correctly claiming these deductions. Additionally, maintaining accurate records of these expenses is vital to substantiate your deductions in the event of an audit.

Business Bank Account and Credit Card

If you have an LLC, there are many advantages to opening a business bank account and obtaining a business credit card. We'll discuss these benefits here, as well as offer some practical guidance for acquiring your new business bank account and credit card with ease.

Advantages of a Business Bank Account

Separation of Finances

Keeping your business finances separate from your personal finances makes it easier to track income, expenses, and deductions. This separation is essential for accurate recordkeeping and tax reporting.

Legal Protection

Separating business and personal finances can help protect personal assets in the event of business-related liabilities or legal issues. This is especially important for notaries and LSAs who handle sensitive documents.

Access to Business Loans

A business bank account can be a prerequisite for securing business loans, lines of credit, or other financial resources that can help your business grow.

Expense Tracking

Business bank accounts often provide detailed monthly statements, making it easier to track business expenses. This simplifies tax preparation and financial management.

Merchant Services

With a business account, you can usually access merchant services, allowing you to accept various forms of payment from clients, including credit card payments.

Advantages of a Business Credit Card

Expenses Separation

A business credit card keeps business expenses separate from personal expenses, simplifying bookkeeping and financial management.

Cash Flow Management

Business credit cards can help with cash flow by providing a revolving credit line. This can be particularly useful for covering business expenses before client payments come in.

Rewards and Perks

Many business credit cards offer rewards, such as cashback or travel rewards, which can provide cost savings and additional benefits for your business.

Credit Building

Using a business credit card responsibly can help build your business credit score. A good credit score is essential when you're applying for loans or financing.

If you're not familiar with building business credit, *The Insider's Guide to Business Credit Using an EIN Only* will teach you the exact steps to access your business credit reports, set up your business credit profile, and achieve the ideal score with each of the three major credit bureaus.

Emergency Funding

In emergencies, a business credit card can provide quick access to funds, which can be a lifeline in the event of unexpected business expenses without disrupting operations.

Purchase Protection

Some business credit cards offer purchase protection, which can be valuable if you make significant business-related purchases.

Before you open a business bank account and credit card, be sure to compare fees, interest rates, and any rewards or perks to make informed decisions that benefit your business. Additionally, always use these financial tools responsibly to maintain a positive financial profile.

Opening a Business Bank Account

- **Choose a bank.** Choose a bank that offers business banking services and has convenient branch locations or online options.

- **Gather the required documents.** Prepare the necessary documents, which typically include your EIN, business formation documents (e.g., articles of organization for an LLC), and personal identification (driver's license or passport).
- **Visit the bank.** Schedule an appointment with the bank or visit a local branch. Bring the required documents with you.
- **Meet with a bank representative.** During your meeting with a bank representative, you will complete the necessary account application. They will guide you through the process and discuss the account options available.
- **Fund the account.** You will need to deposit an initial sum of money into your new business account to open it. This deposit requirement varies by bank and the type of account you choose.
- **Receive account information.** Once your account is open, you will receive your account details, including your account number and routing number. These are essential for processing transactions and setting up payment methods.

Obtaining a Business Credit Card

- **Research credit card options.** Explore business credit card options offered by various financial institutions. Consider factors like interest rates, annual fees, rewards, and credit limits. A few options that are great for small businesses include Ink Business Unlimited from Chase and Blue Business Plus from American Express.

- **Apply for a business credit card.** Visit the financial institution's website or contact them to apply for a business credit card. Complete the credit card application, providing the required information and documentation.
- **Credit evaluation.** The bank or credit card issuers will evaluate your creditworthiness and the credit profile of your business. This may include a credit check and a review of your business's financial health.
- **Review and accept the financial terms.** If your application is approved, carefully review the terms and conditions of the credit card, including interest rates, fees, rewards, and credit limits.
- **Receive and activate the card.** Upon approval, you will receive your business credit card. The issuer will provide you with instructions on how to activate the card.
- **Use responsibly.** Use your business credit card responsibly, making payments on time and in full. Make an effort to limit your utilization to 30% of your available credit.

Tax Season

As a notary public and loan signing agent, your primary focus throughout the year will be serving clients and growing your business. The intricacies of tax season can seem like a maze, but we have your back! In this section, we'll provide invaluable tips and strategies that will help you streamline and simplify your business taxes.

Tracking Expenses and Profits

Keeping detailed records of your expenses and profits is a fundamental practice that can save you time and stress when tax season arrives.

Here's how to do it:

- **Create a spreadsheet.** Set up a dedicated spreadsheet for your business finances. You can use software like Microsoft Excel or Google Sheets for this purpose.
- **Record all transactions.** Enter every business expense and income source into the spreadsheet. Include dates, descriptions, and amounts for each entry. Categorize them to make tracking easier.
- **Regular updates.** Update your spreadsheet regularly, ideally as soon as a transaction occurs. This will help you avoid the hassle of backtracking when preparing for your taxes.
- **Backup documentation.** Keep copies of invoices, receipts, and bank statements as supporting documentation. These will be invaluable if you face an audit or need to clarify any expenses.
- **Organization.** Keep all financial records in a secure and organized manner. Digital storage can be a convenient and space-saving option.

Good recordkeeping is not just a regulatory requirement; it's a smart business practice that can help you save money and protect your financial interests.

Additional Tips for Tax Season

- **Quarterly Taxes:** If your business generates a significant income, consider making quarterly estimated tax payments to avoid underpayment penalties. Consult with a tax professional to determine the appropriate estimated tax amounts.

- **Tax benefits:** Keeping your financial records up-to-date is not just about meeting tax requirements but also about maximizing tax benefits. With accurate records, you can claim eligible deductions and potentially reduce your tax liability.
- **Charitable Contributions:** If your business makes donations to charitable organizations, keep records of these contributions. They can be deductible on your tax return.
- **Accountant or Tax Software:** Consider hiring an accountant for preparing and filing tax returns. It's usually cheaper than you would think and can more than pay for itself. If you're not using an accountant, use a tax software like H&R Block or TurboTax. Both of these have services that provide access to expert help for a nominal fee.

Keep in mind that tax laws and regulations can evolve over time, so it's essential to do your research and stay up-to-date on any changes. Proper tax planning and record-keeping can lead to potential tax savings and a smoother tax season.

Insurance

Errors and omissions (E&O) insurance, also known as professional liability insurance, is a critical safeguard for notaries and LSAs. It offers protection in case of mistakes or oversights made during the notarization or loan signing process. In the event of a claim, this insurance can cover legal expenses, damages, and settlements, helping to protect your assets and business.

The policy minimum is typically $25,000, but it's strongly recommended to consider a higher amount. A policy with $100,000 or more in coverage is often ideal to ensure adequate protection.

E&O insurance can be obtained from various reputable providers. Some recommended insurance companies include Hiscox, Next Insurance, and Travelers. It's advisable to compare quotes and coverage options to find the best fit for your specific needs.

The cost of E&O insurance can vary based on several factors, including coverage amount, location, and individual risk factors. Generally, you can expect to pay an annual premium between $200 to $400. It's an essential investment in your business's financial security and professional reputation.

To ensure comprehensive coverage, carefully review policy details, including coverage limits, deductibles, and any specific exclusions. Discuss your insurance needs with a knowledgeable insurance agent who can guide you in selecting the right policy for your business. By securing adequate E&O insurance, you can operate with confidence and peace of mind, knowing that you're prepared for any unexpected situations that may arise in your profession.

We understand that navigating the complexities of tax obligations and insurance decisions can be challenging, but with the right information and guidance, you can manage these aspects of your business with confidence. By implementing the tips and strategies discussed in this chapter, you can keep your business on the right track and optimize your financial well-being.

Chapter 9

Troubleshooting (Common Pitfalls and How to Avoid Them!)

Every entrepreneurial journey has challenges and obstacles to overcome, and your path to success is no exception. While being a notary and LSA offers flexibility, autonomy, and the potential for substantial income, it's essential to be prepared for the common pitfalls that can arise along the way.

In this chapter, we'll explore issues and roadblocks that many notaries and LSAs may encounter during their careers. In doing so, we'll equip you with the knowledge and strategies needed to proactively tackle these challenges and keep your business thriving.

Common Pitfalls and Strategies to Overcome Them

Pitfall: Irregular Income

This is one of the primary challenges notaries and LSAs may face. Fluctuations in work volume can lead to financial uncertainty. The strategies below will help to mitigate this.

Offer a Range of Services

Consider expanding your service offerings. Notarization services extend beyond real estate transactions and loan signings. You can explore offering additional services like notarizing wills, powers of attorney, affidavits, and more. By diversifying your service portfolio, you can tap into a broader range of client needs and income sources.

Maintain a Reliable Client Base

While attracting new clients is important, don't overlook the value of nurturing your existing client relationships. Building long-term, trusted partnerships with clients can lead to repeat business and referrals. These regular clients provide a steady source of income that helps stabilize your finances.

Partner With Local Businesses

Collaborate with local businesses that require notary services on a regular basis. This can include law firms, real estate agencies, healthcare providers, and financial institutions. Building strategic partnerships with these entities can result in consistent work opportunities. Make sure that these businesses are aware of your services and reliability, which will increase the likelihood of ongoing collaboration.

Explore Mobile Notary Services

Offering mobile notary services allows you to travel to clients' locations, which means convenience and flexibility for you and your clients. This service can cater to a broader range of customers who may require notarization at their homes or workplaces. Mobile notary services often include travel fees, which can contribute to a stable six-figure income. We will discuss offering mobile notary services in more detail in Chapter 11.

Create Service Packages

Consider bundling services or creating service packages that offer added value to your clients. For example, you can offer a complete notary service package for real estate transactions, which includes document notarization, loan signings, and document delivery. Providing packages can lead to increased revenue and a more predictable income stream.

Pitfall: Even Small Mistakes Can Be Costly

Mistakes in the notary and loan signing profession can have significant consequences, both financially and legally. To mitigate this pitfall, you need to take some proactive steps.

Get Training (Even if Not Required)

Training is a fundamental step in becoming a proficient notary and LSA. Even if your state does not mandate formal training, enrolling in reputable notary courses or workshops is highly recommended. These educational programs cover essential notarial practices, legal requirements, and industry best practices. Training will give you the skills and knowledge needed to minimize errors and provide top-notch services.

Stay Up-To-Date With Industry Trends

The notary industry is dynamic, with constantly changing regulations and practices. Joining a notary association, such as the Notary Association of America or the National Notary Association, can be immensely beneficial. Notary associations offer a wealth of resources, including updates on industry trends, access to training courses, and forums for professionals to share their experiences and insights.

Additional benefits of joining a notary association include

- discounts on essential notarial supplies and E&O insurance.
- access to webinars, workshops, and conferences for ongoing education.
- networking opportunities to connect with other notaries and learn from their experiences.
- updates on state-specific laws and regulations to ensure compliance.
- templates and guides for common notarial tasks, ensuring accuracy in your work.

Do Your Research

Never underestimate the power of research. When faced with unfamiliar notarial practices or specific document requirements, invest the time in research to understand the situation thoroughly. Double-check state laws and guidelines, and ensure that you have the most up-to-date information before proceeding with any notarization.

Avoid Offering Legal Advice

It's essential to understand the boundaries of your role as a notary or LSA. Offering legal advice is outside your scope of practice and can lead to facing legal consequences. Instead, focus on providing notarial services and document verification within the parameters of the law.

Get Errors and Omissions Insurance

E&O insurance is a critical component of protecting your professional interests. While some states require it, having E&O insurance is advisable for all notaries and LSAs.

Pitfall: Not Getting Paid

It's important for any business's cash flow to make sure that clients pay in a timely manner. The strategies below will ensure you receive compensation for your work.

Get Paid at the Time (for Notaries)

For standard notary services, particularly those offered in your office or a client's location, it's common and advisable to request payment at the time of service. This practice simplifies the payment process and reduces the likelihood of delayed or missed payments.

Send an Invoice Immediately (for LSAs)

LSAs often don't receive payment at the time of service, as their clients are typically title companies or signing services. In such cases, it's essential to have a clear and organized invoicing system. As soon as the loan signing is complete, send an invoice to your client promptly.

Specify a Clear Due Date

Ensure your invoice includes a specific due date for payment. This due date should be reasonable and reflective of typical industry payment terms. To avoid misunderstandings, make it clear to your clients that payment is due by this date.

Record Unpaid Invoices

Maintain a record of all outstanding invoices and clients who haven't paid within the agreed-upon time frame. This record is a tool for tracking your accounts receivable and ensuring that no payments slip through the cracks.

Implement a Follow-Up System

Create a systematic follow-up process for unpaid invoices. This might include sending an email reminder, making a courtesy call, and escalating communication if necessary. Most clients appreciate a professional reminder, as it can help them manage their accounts more efficiently.

Late Payment Fees and Terms

Your invoice should clearly outline any late payment fees and terms. These terms can serve as an incentive for clients to pay on time. Be transparent about any additional costs incurred due to late payments.

Legal Safeguards

Familiarize yourself with the legal remedies available in your jurisdiction for unpaid invoices. In some cases, you may need to seek legal recourse for unpaid bills, such as small claims court. Having this knowledge can serve as a last resort if all other efforts fail.

Pitfall: Time Management Challenges

Effective time management is essential to make sure that you can handle your workload efficiently. The nature of this profession can be unpredictable, making time management very important. Below are some effective ways to avoid this pitfall.

Create a Daily Schedule

Begin each day with a clear and structured schedule. Allocate specific time blocks for appointments, administrative tasks, marketing efforts, and personal time. Prioritize tasks based on their importance and deadlines. Use digital calendars or physical planners to keep your schedule organized.

Set Boundaries for Work Hours

One common challenge in this profession is the blurring of boundaries between personal and work life. To avoid overworking or becoming overwhelmed, set specific work hours. Communicate these hours to clients, family, and friends to establish expectations and boundaries.

Use Digital Tools

Embrace digital tools and software designed for time management and productivity. Some recommended tools include calendar applications like Google Calendar or Microsoft Outlook, task management apps like Todoist or Trello, and note-taking applications like Evernote. These tools can streamline your tasks and keep you organized.

Prioritize Administrative Tasks

Administrative tasks, like invoicing, recordkeeping, and appointment scheduling, can consume a significant amount of time. Prioritize these tasks and allocate specific blocks for them in your daily schedule. Accounting software and customer relationship management (CRM) tools can simplify these processes.

Outsource

Recognize when certain tasks can be outsourced. For instance, if bookkeeping and accounting consume too much of your time, you may need to think about hiring a professional accountant. This allows you to focus on core business activities while ensuring that financial matters are well-managed.

Minimize Distractions

Identify common distractions in your work environment and take steps to minimize them. These distractions can range from social media to household chores. Create a dedicated workspace free from distractions during work hours. Use website blockers or time-tracking apps to stay on track.

Evaluate and Adjust

Regularly assess your time management strategies to identify what works best for you. Be open to adjustments as your business evolves and your workload changes, so you can continuously improve your efficiency.

Pitfall: Document Errors

Mistakes in documents can lead to legal complications, damage your professional reputation, and inconvenience your clients. To ensure your documents are consistently accurate and error-free, follow the comprehensive fix below.

Implement a Thorough Document Review Process

Before notarizing or handling any document, develop a meticulous review process. This involves carefully examining each document, page by page, to verify the accuracy of all information, signatures, and dates.

Pay particular attention to names, addresses, and legal descriptions. Ensure that all required elements, like notary certificates and jurats, are properly completed. If you detect any discrepancies or incomplete sections, address them promptly with the document issuer or signatories.

Maintain Up-To-Date Knowledge of State-Specific Notarial Requirements

Stay informed about the specific rules and regulations governing notarization in your jurisdiction. Regularly consult your state's notary handbook, attend training sessions or workshops, and join professional notary associations that offer resources and updates. This knowledge will help you understand the unique notarial requirements of your state and avoid any document errors.

Use Software Tools for Document Verification

Leverage technology to enhance the accuracy of your document verification process. Various software tools are available to help notaries and loan signing agents verify the authenticity of documents.

Many tools can also detect potential errors, such as missing signatures, incorrect dates, or incomplete notarial certificates. Just remember to always manually review documents in addition to using software.

Maintain a Detailed Document Log

Create and maintain a comprehensive document log for every transaction you handle. This log should include essential details about the documents you notarize or assist with, such as the date, parties involved, type of document, and notarial act performed. A document log serves as a valuable reference in case questions or disputes arise about a specific transaction.

Double-Check High-Risk Documents

Certain documents, like legal contracts or financial agreements, carry a higher risk if errors are present. Double-check these high-risk documents, even if it means a more thorough review process. Confirm that all parties involved fully understand the contents of the document before notarization.

Collaborate With Document Issuers

Maintain open communication with the document issuers and signatories. Clarify any ambiguities or discrepancies you encounter during the document review process. Address potential errors directly with the parties involved to rectify issues before notarization.

Document Training and Continuing Education

Invest in ongoing training and education to stay updated on best practices for document review. Many notary associations and industry organizations offer courses and workshops focused on document accuracy and thorough review process.

Pitfall: Fee Negotiations

Fee negotiations can be challenging, but they are a part of any business. Clients may have different expectations or budget constraints, particularly when it comes to loan signing services. Below are some ideas for effectively handling fee negotiations.

Transparent Pricing

Begin by setting clear and transparent pricing for your notary and loan signing services. Make sure your pricing structure is well-defined and easy for clients to understand. Avoid hidden fees or additional charges that could lead to misunderstandings.

Communicate Fees Clearly

When you discuss your fees with potential clients, do so in a professional and courteous manner. Present a well-structured fee schedule that outlines the costs associated with your services. Offer clients a written estimate that includes a breakdown of fees.

Provide a Professional Quote

In cases where a potential client requests a quote for your services, prepare a professional document that clearly specifies the scope of work, associated costs, and any potential additional charges. This will serve as a reference point during negotiations.

Be Prepared to Negotiate

Understand that clients may seek to negotiate fees, especially if they have specific budget constraints. Be open to negotiation while maintaining your commitment to providing high-quality services.

Prior to the negotiation, establish your "bottom line," or the minimum fee you are willing to accept. This ensures you do not compromise your business profitability.

Identify Nonnegotiables

During negotiations, determine which aspects of the fee structure are nonnegotiable. For example, if certain services involve significant travel time or additional expenses, you may need to maintain firm pricing on these aspects. Clearly communicate which elements of the fee structure can be adjusted and which cannot.

Understand Client Budgets

Gain insights into your client's budget constraints and limitations. By understanding their financial situation, you can tailor your negotiation strategy to find a mutually beneficial solution.

Offer Value in Negotiations

When negotiating fees, focus on the value you provide to clients. Highlight the benefits of your services, your expertise, and your commitment to professionalism. Emphasize how your services can save clients time, reduce risks, and ensure legal compliance. This approach can justify your fees and enhance your negotiating position.

Written Agreements

After successful fee negotiations, make sure that all agreed-upon terms are documented in a written agreement or contract. This written record protects both you and the client by preventing misunderstandings or disputes.

Professional Demeanor

Maintain professionalism and a positive demeanor throughout fee negotiations. Respect the client's perspective, even if an agreement cannot be reached. A courteous and professional approach can leave a positive impression, which may lead to future business opportunities.

Reevaluate Pricing Periodically

Periodically reevaluate your pricing structure to make sure that it aligns with market trends and your business's financial goals. Adjust your fees as necessary while maintaining a balance between profitability and client satisfaction.

By identifying and addressing potential stumbling blocks, you are better equipped to provide reliable services, maintain your professional reputation, and build lasting client relationships. As you move forward, keep in mind that learning from these pitfalls is an essential part of your growth as a notary and LSA.

In Part III of the book, we'll explore how to diversify your business, scale it to six figures, and achieve long-term success in the industry. Your journey is just beginning, and the possibilities are vast. Stay motivated, stay informed, and stay committed to the path you've chosen. Success is within your reach!

Part Three

Expand Your Business to Six Figures

Chapter 10

Diversify for $$$

In your journey to becoming a successful notary public and LSA, diversifying your services is a pivotal strategy that can pave the way for massive growth and six-figure earnings.

This chapter delves into the importance of offering a variety of services and how it can contribute to building a thriving and resilient business. We'll provide a full list of exciting and profitable new services you can add to your growing notary public and LSA business to reach six figures with ease.

The Power of Diversification

Diversification isn't just a buzzword; it's an important approach to ensuring your business's sustainability and financial stability. By expanding the range of services you provide, you create multiple income streams, reducing the risk associated with relying solely on a single service.

In other words, if the demand for one of your services decreases, you'll still have other services to fall back on. This diversification is akin to building a sturdy bridge, where each service serves as a supporting pillar, reinforcing your business structure.

One of the significant advantages of diversifying your services is the ability to set your own fees. As you add more services to your repertoire, you gain the flexibility to determine the pricing for each service. This means that you have the power to increase your income by offering services at competitive rates in your state. The versatility of your fee structure can be a potent tool for scaling your income as you cater to a broader clientele with varying budgets and needs.

It's important to stress that when setting your fees, you should always conduct thorough research to ensure your rates align with industry standards and any set fees in your state. Competitive pricing ensures that your services remain attractive to clients while allowing you to maintain profitability.

It's also vital to remember that the regulations and laws governing notary public and LSA services can vary significantly from one state to the next. As a diligent business owner, it's your responsibility to understand the specific requirements of your state before offering any of the diversified services outlined in this chapter.

In sum, diversifying your services is a strategic move that can transform your notary and LSA business. It opens doors to new opportunities, increases your earning potential, and provides a safety net in times of fluctuating demand.

Diversified Services for Notaries and LSAs

In the upcoming sections, we'll explore various services that you can incorporate into your business, alongside valuable tips and insights for each one. Your journey to a thriving and diversified business begins here, as you explore the multifaceted world of notary and loan signing services.

Courier or Document Delivery Service

This service involves securely delivering important documents, contracts, or paperwork from one location to another. Clients often seek out this service when time-sensitive deliveries are crucial or when they require a reliable and trustworthy courier for sensitive documents.

Here are some tips for successfully incorporating courier or document delivery services into your business:

- Emphasize the security of your document delivery service. Assure clients that their documents will be handled with the utmost care and confidentiality.
- Invest in secure and tamper-proof document transportation methods, such as lockable bags or boxes, to ensure the safety and privacy of the documents during transit.
- Check your state's regulations regarding courier services. Depending on the state, certain requirements or licenses may be necessary for this type of service.

Remember to prioritize security, reliability, and professionalism to build a strong reputation as a trusted courier for important documents.

Process Server

This service involves delivering legal documents, like subpoenas, summonses, and court orders to individuals involved in legal proceedings. Process servers play a crucial role in making sure that due process is followed in legal matters.

Here are some tips for successfully incorporating process serving into your business:

- As a process server, you must remain neutral and impartial. Your role is to deliver legal documents and not to become involved in the legal case itself.
- Familiarize yourself with your state's specific legal requirements for process servers. This may include licensing, training, and legal restrictions.
- Serve the legal documents to the intended recipients in a timely manner. Promptness is often critical in legal proceedings.
- Effectively communicate with your clients about the progress of service, any challenges encountered, and when service has been successfully completed.
- Make sure you comprehend the legal process and that you adhere to it strictly. You should also have an understanding of the different types of documents.
- In some cases, recipients of legal documents may react negatively or be uncooperative. Be prepared to handle such situations professionally and within the boundaries of the law.
- Given the potential for legal challenges in process serving, having professional liability insurance can provide protection in case of legal disputes.
- Build relationships with local attorneys and legal firms. They often require reliable process servers and can become a valuable source of clients.

Adding process serving to your repertoire can be a valuable extension of your notary and loan signing agent business. However, it's vital to approach this service with a proper understanding of legal requirements, professionalism, and commitment to maintaining impartiality. By providing a reliable service, you can serve the legal community and generate additional income.

Mobile Exam Proctor

Offering a mobile exam proctor service means facilitating and supervising exams for individuals or institutions at various locations. This service is especially useful for students, professionals, or organizations seeking flexibility in taking exams outside traditional testing centers.

Here are some tips for successfully incorporating mobile exam proctoring into your business:

- Research your state's regulations regarding exam proctoring and ensure compliance with any specific requirements or licensing. In some cases, proctors may need certification.
- Each exam may have specific rules and guidelines. It's important to thoroughly understand these rules and communicate them to the test-takers.
- Make sure to protect the integrity and security of the exam by following the established procedures for check-in, monitoring, and reporting any irregularities.
- Familiarize yourself with the testing software or platforms being used, as different exams may have varying technological requirements. Be prepared to assist test-takers in troubleshooting common issues.
- Confirm the identity of each test-taker using government-issued photo identification and any additional verification methods required by the testing agency.
- Establish clear terms and conditions for your proctoring service, including fees, cancellation policies, and any additional services you may offer.

- Build relationships with educational institutions, online learning platforms, and professional organizations to expand your network and client base.

Mobile exam proctoring is a service that caters to the growing demand for flexible testing solutions, and you can assist students and professionals in achieving their educational goals while earning additional income.

Apostille Agent

Apostille agents play a vital role in the process of legalizing documents for international use. Their services involve obtaining and verifying apostilles, which are specialized certificates that authenticate the legitimacy of documents, making them valid and recognized in foreign countries.

Here are some tips for successfully incorporating apostille services into your business:

- Familiarize yourself with the Hague Convention and the specific requirements for obtaining an apostille. Each country may have its own rules and procedures.
- While not required in all cases, having a legal background or expertise in document authentication may be needed for each document type.
- Different types of documents may require apostilles, including birth certificates, marriage licenses, academic transcripts, and more. You will need to understand the specific needs of each document type.
- Establish connections with government agencies, embassies, and consulates, as these entities are often involved in the apostille process. Having a network can expedite the process.

- The apostille process often involves deadlines, particularly for international travel or legal matters. You will need to be prompt and make sure that clients receive their apostilled documents within the required time frame.
- While you will be involved in obtaining and verifying the apostille, you will not be responsible for issuing it. This is done by a state agency, usually the Secretary of State's office.

By offering this specialized service, you can assist clients in navigating the complex world of document legalization and international legal processes while generating extra income.

Printing Services

This service involves providing clients with document printing solutions, which can include contracts, forms, legal paperwork, and more. This service is especially helpful for clients who require physical copies of important documents.

Here are some tips for successfully incorporating printing services into your business:

- To provide professional printing services, invest in high-quality printing equipment. Make sure that your printer can produce clear and legible documents, especially for legal and contractual paperwork.
- Offer a range of paper options to cater to different client preferences and document requirements. This can include standard letter-sized, legal-sized paper, or specialty paper for official documents.
- Exercise caution and professionalism when handling sensitive documents. Make sure that documents are properly collated and organized before printing.

- Promote your printing services to your existing client base as an additional convenience. Tell them about the advantages of one-stop document services.

Adding printing services to your repertoire can streamline the document-handling process, making sure that clients have all their needs met in one place.

Field Inspector

Field inspectors are responsible for conducting property inspections, typically for real estate, insurance, or financial purposes. These inspections involve documenting the condition, occupancy, and various attributes of a property.

Here are some tips for successfully incorporating field inspecting into your business:

- Depending on your state's regulations, you may need specific licensing or certification to perform field inspections. Ensure that you meet these requirements before offering the service.
- Market your services to local real estate agents, insurance companies, lenders, and property management firms. These businesses often require field inspection services.
- Field inspections involve visiting properties, which can carry risks. Obtain the necessary insurance coverage to protect yourself in case of accidents or incidents during inspections.
- Invest in the tools required for field inspections, such as a camera, measuring devices, a flashlight, and forms for recording property details.
- Create a standardized system for documenting property conditions, taking photographs, and filling out inspection reports. Accurate and detailed records are essential.

- Timely reporting is critical in the field inspection business. Make sure that you deliver inspection reports and findings promptly to clients.
- Pay close attention to details during property inspections. Accurate and thorough reports are crucial for your clients.

Field inspections are in demand for various industries, and your expertise in handling documents can position you as a reliable field inspector in your area.

Wedding Officiant

As a wedding officiant, you will have the honor of officiating wedding ceremonies, which can be a deeply fulfilling and joyful part of your work.

Here are some tips for successfully incorporating wedding officiant services into your business:

- Research the legal requirements for becoming a wedding officiant in your state; some states may require specific registration or authorization.
- Understand the legal aspects of marriage licenses. Make sure you follow state laws and requirements for officiating weddings.
- Determine your fees for wedding officiant services. Fees can be based on factors like ceremony complexity, location, and your level of involvement.
- Become active in the wedding community and network with local wedding planners, photographers, and venues to expand your reach. Encourage couples to provide reviews and testimonials after their wedding ceremonies.
- Consider attending workshops or courses on wedding ceremony design and officiating to enhance your skills.

Your experience in handling official documents and ensuring the legality of transactions can enhance the trust couples have in your role as their wedding officiant. It's a rewarding way to expand your business and income while making a meaningful impact on people's lives.

Authorized Representative for Form I-9

Being an authorized representative for Form I-9 allows you to assist employers with verifying the eligibility and identity of new hires. Note that this service is distinct from notarization and focuses on compliance with employment eligibility requirements.

Here are some tips for successfully incorporating Form I-9 services into your business:

- Consider enrolling in training courses related to I-9 compliance and authorized representative duties to ensure you understand the legal requirements.
- Keep clear and accurate records of all components of Form I-9 for review. This is essential for compliance and potential audits.
- Promote your services to local businesses, especially those that frequently hire new employees.

Your professional expertise and attention to detail can make the I-9 verification process smoother for both employers and potential employees.

Mobile Finger Printing

Adding mobile fingerprinting services to your notary public and loan signing agent roles offers a convenient solution for individuals and organizations requiring fingerprinting for various purposes, including background checks, licensing, and security clearance.

Here are some tips for successfully incorporating mobile finger printing into your business:

- Be sure to understand the fingerprinting process, including the equipment and technology involved as well as legal requirements.
- Invest in high-quality equipment, like electronic fingerprint scanners, ink pads, and fingerprint cards.
- Offer flexible scheduling options for clients, as some may require fingerprinting services outside of regular business hours.
- Prioritize the privacy and security of clients' personal information and fingerprints. Implement data protection measures and establish secure storage practices.
- Make sure that you meet any necessary requirements to conduct background checks if that service is included in your offerings.

With proper training and adherence to legal regulations, you can provide a sought-after service that meets the increasing demand for fingerprinting in various industries, including law enforcement, healthcare, and professional licensing.

Immigration Forms Specialist

This service involves assisting individuals with completing and submitting various immigration-related forms, like green card and citizenship applications. In doing so, you'll help clients effectively navigate the complex immigration process.

Here are some tips for successfully incorporating immigration forms services into your business:

- Your primary purpose is to help clients complete immigration forms and prepare packages for submission to United States Citizenship and Immigration Services (USCIS). This can include offering additional services, such as translating the client's answers onto the forms.

- You will often need to help clients collect birth certificates or other vital records needed to complete the immigration process. Make sure they understand your role is to assist with form completion, not provide legal advice.
- While you won't be providing legal advice, it's still important that you have a solid understanding of immigration laws and regulations. Be sure to stay up-to-date with any changes to immigration policies.

By ensuring accurate and well-prepared forms, you play a crucial role in helping clients achieve their immigration goals.

Permit Runner Service

Offering permit runner services involves helping individuals or businesses navigate the permit application process for a number of purposes, like construction permits, business licenses, or event permits. Permit runners act as intermediaries between clients and local government agencies, streamlining the application process.

Here are some tips for successfully incorporating permit runner services into your business:

- Gain a comprehensive understanding of local, state, and federal regulations governing permits and licenses relevant to your service area.
- Assist clients in gathering all required documentation for permit applications, including forms, plans, and fees. Verify the completeness of the application packages.
- It's important to establish relationships with local government offices and agencies responsible for permit

processing. Familiarity with key contacts can expedite the application process.

- Tailor your services to meet the unique needs of each client, whether they are applying for construction permits, business licenses, or event permits.

Permit runner services can be a lucrative addition to your current business, as they require a minimum outlay with no special equipment.

Advance Directive Notarizations

Many hospitals and hospices request an advance healthcare directive before major surgical procedures or when patients need to make end-of-life decisions. Critical medical documents, like medical power of attorney and living wills, may require notary services, depending on the state.

Here are some tips for successfully incorporating advance directive notarizations into your business:

- Understand the different healthcare documents, their purposes, and the legal requirements for notarization.
- These services need to be handled with compassion, care, and sympathy, as clients may be facing challenging medical decisions.
- Ensure that clients can reach you in critical moments. You may need to be available for notarizations during nonstandard business hours if necessary.

Your expertise in providing healthcare notarizations provides peace of mind to clients, ensuring their medical wishes are legally documented and honored, even in difficult times.

When expanding your notary public and loan signing agent business, it's essential to approach it strategically. To start, select one or two services from the additional offerings provided that align best with your strengths, interests, and local demand.

You can even conduct a poll on social media or via email to gauge your clients' preferences. Prioritize services that are convenient for you to perform and align well with your current client base.

Once you're ready to introduce these new services, market them effectively. Send out an email blast to your contact list, create engaging social media posts, and update your website to inform potential and existing clients. To attract initial interest, consider offering introductory discounts. For instance, a 30% discount during the first week of launch can entice clients to give your new services a try.

Encourage clients who have experienced your new services to provide testimonials or referrals. Positive feedback will enhance your reputation and trustworthiness as an expert in these areas.

By starting with a strategic approach and gradually expanding your service offerings, you can effectively grow your notary and loan signing business, cater to diverse client needs, and build a strong reputation in these additional service areas. This steady progression will lead to long-term success in your expanding venture.

Chapter 11

Scale to Six Figures

Welcome to the chapter that holds the keys to scaling your income as a notary public and LSA to the coveted six-figure mark. It's exciting, isn't it?

In the following pages, we're going to unveil straightforward strategies that can rapidly elevate your earnings. And the best part? These methods won't demand an avalanche of clients or an overwhelming increase in your workload. Whether you're dedicated to your business full-time or juggling it with a few weekly hours, the four powerful strategies we'll explore here will set your income trajectory soaring.

Earning a six-figure income might seem like a distant dream, but it's well within your grasp. All it takes is a strategic approach and a willingness to implement these techniques.

So, let's find out how you can chart your path to financial success in the world of notary and loan signing services. Your journey to six figures begins now!

Mobile Notary

A mobile notary, sometimes referred to as a traveling notary, is a notary public who provides services on the go. Instead of clients coming to their office, mobile notaries travel to the client's location to perform notarial acts. This flexibility and convenience have made mobile notaries increasingly popular.

The heightened demand for mobile notary services, coupled with the ability to charge travel-related fees, creates a significantly higher income potential. In addition, mobile notaries don't require an office space, which greatly reduces overhead costs, resulting in a higher overall profit margin.

Clients appreciate the convenience of mobile notaries, especially when they have busy schedules or specific mobility issues that make it challenging to visit a notary's office. By offering on-site services, mobile notaries cater to their clients' needs, creating a more customer-friendly experience while expanding the profit potential of their client base.

How to Become a Mobile Notary

The requirements for becoming a mobile notary are generally the same as those for becoming a traditional notary public. There are, however, some additional considerations when becoming a mobile notary. Let's have a look at them:

- **Travel expenses:** You'll need to factor in travel-related expenses when setting your fees. This may include mileage, parking, fuel, and any other costs associated with reaching your clients. Some states have set travel fees for mobile notaries, so make sure you're aware of those before calculating costs.

- **Transportation:** To operate as a mobile notary, you'll need a reliable vehicle to travel to your clients' locations. Ensure your vehicle is well-maintained and properly insured.
- **Scheduling flexibility:** As a mobile notary, you should be prepared to work outside regular business hours, as clients might require notarizations during the evenings or weekends.
- **Travel time:** Account for the time it takes to travel to and from client locations when scheduling appointments. Consider travel time when setting your fees.
- **Background checks:** Some states may require background checks for mobile notaries, especially if they are providing services in sensitive areas like healthcare or law enforcement facilities.
- **Carry essential supplies:** Make sure you have all necessary notary supplies, including a notary stamp or seal, a notary journal, and any other tools required to perform notarizations while on the go.

It's important to check with your Secretary of State's office to understand any state-specific requirements for mobile notaries.

Helpful Tips

- Travel costs and expenses, such as fuel, maintenance, and parking fees, should be carefully calculated before a fee is agreed upon.
- There may be safety concerns if you're traveling to unfamiliar locations. Prioritize your safety and inform a trusted family member or friend about your whereabouts.

- No-show clients can be mitigated by implementing a clear cancellation policy and potentially requesting payment of travel fees in advance (if your state allows it).

Remote Online Notary (RON)

A remote online notary (RON) is a notary public who can notarize documents using online technology, typically over a secure video conferencing platform. RON services have become increasingly popular due to their convenience and efficiency, especially in a world where digital transactions are on the rise.

RONs conduct notarizations remotely, using electronic signature-related technologies alongside industry-standard video conferencing technology. The notary and the client are in different locations but can see and interact with each other through a secure video link.

Documentation is digital, the signer's identity is verified online, and electronic copies of the document are notarized. Clients typically upload their documents to the RON's platform, where the notary performs the notarization virtually.

RONs offer even greater convenience and flexibility compared to mobile notaries. They can serve clients located anywhere, as long as they can connect through a video conference. This extends their reach nationally and even internationally resulting in higher income potential.

RON services have evolved to meet the demands of the modern, digital world. They are especially useful for notarizing documents across long distances or during situations where in-person meetings are challenging. RONs complement the services of mobile notaries, offering clients a broader range of options for notarizing documents while expanding business opportunities for notaries themselves.

Benefits of Offering RON Services

- **Convenience and flexibility:** You can work from home and set your own working hours. Working from home also means that you don't need to travel, which gives you more time to book additional appointments.
- **Higher earning potential:** The state fee limits for RONs can be significantly higher, which equates to more income per notarization.
- **Faster than traditional notarizations:** This means you can perform more notarizations in less time, which leads to a higher income without increasing your hours.

How to Become a RON

- **Check your eligibility.** Ensure you meet the eligibility requirements set by your state. These requirements can vary, but they often include being a commissioned notary public and completing additional training. Please note that while most states have adopted permanent RON laws, in several other states, it's only allowed temporarily or not at all. If you live in a state that doesn't currently allow RON, be sure to stay up-to-date on RON laws, as this could change in the future.
- **Complete training.** Sign up for any required RON training programs or courses. Training typically covers the rules and technology used in online notarization. We recommend this short training from the National Notary

Association: nationalnotary.org/remote-online-notary-education.

- **Choose a RON platform.** Select a RON platform or technology provider. Many notaries opt to work with established RON platforms like Notarize.com, DocVerify, or Pavaso. These platforms provide the technology and infrastructure needed for remote online notarizations.

- **Install the necessary software.** Install the required software for online notarization. This may include video conferencing tools, digital notary stamps, and secure document-sharing platforms.

- **Do the verification process.** You will need to verify the identity of the signer remotely. This often involves using a combination of knowledge-based authentication, biometrics, and government-issued ID verification.

- **Perform RONs.** With the technology and processes in place, you can start performing remote online notarizations. Clients can connect with you online to have their documents notarized.

- **Maintain compliance.** Make sure you adhere to all the regulations and requirements specific to your state. This includes keeping records of your remote notarizations and following any state-specific guidelines.

Recommended RON Platforms

- **Notarize.com** offers a comprehensive platform for online notarizations, with tools for both notaries and clients.

- **PandaDoc** includes eNotary functionality as part of its document management and electronic signature platform.
- **DocVerify** is a cloud-based electronic notarization platform designed for notaries and businesses.
- **Pavaso** offers an end-to-end digital closing platform, which includes RON capabilities for notaries and mortgage professionals.

Please note that many of these RON platforms are only available in certain states. It's important to do your own research to determine which platform is best for your location and business.

After-Hours or Holiday Services

Offering after-hours or holiday services is a smart strategic move that can result in a significant income boost. You'll work the same amount of hours, but increase your earnings by simply shifting your availability.

There's a growing demand for notary, signing, and related services around the clock. Many situations require notarizations or signings outside of regular business hours. For example, people may need a power of attorney notarized late at night in a medical emergency, or they might require a document notarized during a holiday to close a real estate deal.

By offering services during off-hours, you tap into this demand and can sometimes even charge an additional fee (depending on the service) for convenience. This creates the potential to make more income for the same amount of time and effort.

By providing services during these times, you face less competition from other notary businesses. This translates to a higher likelihood of receiving new clients and additional income.

Even in today's digital age, many people still turn to traditional sources like banks or credit unions for notary services. When these institutions are closed during off-hours or holidays, you have a significant opportunity to become the go-to choice in your area. By being open when others are not, you can capture a substantial share of the market and build a strong reputation as a reliable and available notary.

This can be especially effective if you're only working on your business a few hours a week. The flexibility allows you to serve clients outside your regular working hours, effectively turning your part-time venture into a high-income side hustle.

To make the most of this strategy, it's crucial to advertise your after-hours and holiday services prominently. Feature this information on your website, email communications, and social media. Let potential clients know that you are available when others may not be. This will attract clients looking for your specific availability and grow your business's profitability.

Work With Escrow Officers

Collaborating with escrow officers is a strategic move that can greatly benefit LSAs. Escrow officers often pay higher fees per signing appointment compared to standard loan signing services.

While loan signing services typically pay $75 to $125 per signing appointment, escrow officers may pay $125 to $200 or more for each signing. This higher fee per appointment can significantly boost your income without requiring any extra time or effort.

When you collaborate with an escrow officer, you typically keep 100% of the signing fee. In contrast, when working through a signing service, you may have to split the fee with the service. By partnering directly with an escrow officer, you maximize your earnings for each signing appointment.

The demand for loan signings and related services is generally high in the real estate industry. Many escrow officers work with a minimum of five to ten signing agents to meet the needs of their clients. They often have numerous signing appointments throughout the day and require LSAs who can accommodate different schedules. This high demand provides ample opportunities for LSAs to secure business by working directly with escrow officers.

How to Get Started

If you're interested in collaborating with escrow officers, below are a couple of effective ways to get started.

- **Direct outreach:** You can search for escrow companies in your local area and reach out directly to these firms. Contact their escrow officers or signing departments and introduce yourself and your services. Highlight your qualifications and emphasize the convenience of direct collaboration.
- **Real estate agent referrals:** Another effective approach is to ask real estate agents, especially those who know you well or have worked with you before, to recommend your services to escrow officers. Real estate agents often have strong connections with escrow professionals and can vouch for your reliability and expertise. A referral from a trusted real estate agent can go a long way in securing direct partnerships with escrow officers.

By working directly with escrow officers, you can establish strong partnerships in the real estate industry. This collaboration allows you to leverage your skills and expertise to provide valuable services to clients while maximizing your earnings. As you embrace innovative strategies and expand your service offerings, you'll find yourself paving a fast track to financial success.

This chapter has outlined some of the most effective methods to boost your income to six figures without overextending your workload. Pair these with the diversification strategies in Chapter 10 and your income will soar faster than you could ever imagine!

This power to skyrocket your earnings lies within your grasp, whether you're working on your business part-time or full-time. By applying the principles and techniques outlined here, you can effectively achieve your financial goals and unlock the limitless potential of your notary and LSA business.

Chapter 12

Insider Secrets for Success

Welcome to the chapter where we unlock the vault of insider secrets for success in the notarization and signing business. If you've come this far, you've undoubtedly recognized the potential for a rewarding and prosperous career as a notary and LSA. But success isn't built overnight; it's a long-term endeavor. To reap the full benefits of your investment in this profession, you must commit to a vision that extends beyond the present moment.

As a notary public and LSA, your aspiration is to create a sustainable enterprise that continually enriches your life through increasing income and professional satisfaction. We understand that, which is why this section is dedicated to guiding you along that path to enduring success. In this chapter, we'll unveil five important actions that, when practiced consistently, will virtually ensure the growth and prosperity of your business.

Remember, success is not a sprint; it is a marathon. It's a journey filled with lessons, growth, and persistence. You have a solid foundation for your six-figure business. Now, let's construct the framework for sustainable, long-term success as a notary public and LSA.

Secret #1: Client Retention Is Key

Client retention is one of the cornerstones of success in the notarization and signing business, and it's crucial for building a flourishing long-term enterprise.

According to research, increasing client retention by just 5% can increase your company's profitability by a whopping 75%. This number alone should show you the critical role that client retention plays in expanding your notary and LSA firm.

So, how can you build great relationships with your clients to make sure that they come back to you time and time again? Here are some great strategies:

Gratitude Is Golden

One effective way to nurture your relationships with clients is by expressing your gratitude. Thank-you notes, holiday cards, follow-up emails, and greeting cards can go a long way. These small gestures of appreciation show your clients that you value their business and, more importantly, their trust. By acknowledging their loyalty, you can encourage repeat business and build a relationship that goes beyond the transactional nature of your services.

Ask for Referrals

One of the most powerful forms of marketing is word-of-mouth. People trust personal recommendations above all else. If your clients are satisfied with your services, consider asking them for referrals.

According to research, consumers are 77% more likely to purchase a good or service if a friend recommends it. So, let your clients know that their recommendations can be the best gift they give you. Their endorsement can bring new clients to your door.

Loyalty Rewards

Building loyalty is a two-way street. As a token of your appreciation, offer incentives to regular customers. Consider offering discounted or even occasional complimentary notarizations as a thank you. This not only strengthens your relationship with current clients but also encourages them to continue doing business with you. Loyalty programs, periodic discounts, or special packages for returning customers can all be helpful methods for keeping your client base strong.

Your clients are the most important asset in your business. By focusing on client retention, you not only boost your company's revenue but also build a supportive community of happy clients.

Remember that keeping your clients satisfied, engaged, and loyal is more than simply a business plan; it's a dedication to providing the best service possible and encouraging lasting success in your notary and LSA endeavor. In an era where gaining a new customer can cost up to five times more than retaining an existing one, it's clear that client retention is the key to long-term profitability.

Secret #2: Networking Is Gold

In the notary and LSA industry, networking is the catalyst that can propel your business to new heights. It opens doors, creates opportunities, and nurtures lasting professional relationships. This is a people-driven business and the more connections you have, the more successful you'll be in the long run.

Here are some effective strategies to make networking work for you:

Conferences and Workshops

Attending industry-specific conferences and workshops is a fantastic way to expand your professional network. These events bring together like-minded individuals who are passionate about notarization and signing services.

A few recommendations include the NNA Annual Conference, the Loan Signing System's National Conference, or local real estate and legal workshops. These gatherings offer an opportunity to collaborate, learn, and build connections.

Local Chamber of Commerce

Consider joining your local Chamber of Commerce. This membership can provide you with ample opportunities to meet with local businesses, professionals, and potential clients. It's a great avenue to strengthen your reputation in the community and build relationships that can lead to more business.

Notary Associations

Joining a notary association, like the American Association of Notaries or the Notary Association of America, is another excellent strategy. As discussed previously, these associations offer numerous benefits, including networking opportunities, access to valuable resources, educational materials, and even discounts.

Local Notary Groups

In addition to formal associations, it's worth seeking out or creating local notary groups. Connect with notaries in your area, both physically and virtually, through social media groups, forums, or local meet-up events. You can often find these groups on Meetup or LinkedIn.

By engaging with your fellow notaries, you can share experiences and gain insights into industry trends that will improve your overall business. As a bonus, other notaries may even refer clients to you when they are busy or out of town. This collaboration is mutually beneficial and can bolster your credibility and client base.

Keep in mind that networking extends beyond just meeting people; it's about fostering lasting connections. In all your interactions, maintain a high level of professionalism. Approach networking with a genuine intention to collaborate and learn from colleagues. It's not just about what others can do for you but also what you can bring to the table. This approach creates a win-win situation that leads to meaningful connections.

By attending industry events, joining local organizations, and connecting with fellow notaries, you create opportunities that can lead to increased income and a more rewarding career. The true power of networking lies not just in the number of connections you make but in the quality of the relationships you build. Your network is your net worth!

Secret #3: Learning Is Growth

In any career, mastery and improvement go hand in hand with knowledge and learning. The notarization and signing business is no exception.

The more you learn about the industry and hone your skills, the better you'll become at your craft. This continuous learning process offers several substantial benefits that can significantly contribute to your business success. This includes smoother and faster appointments, a robust professional reputation, higher pay for certain services, and more.

Here are some strategies for incorporating continuous learning into your notary and LSA business:

Adaption to Industry Changes

The legal and real estate industries are constantly evolving. New regulations, technologies, and market trends emerge regularly. Staying updated through continuous learning ensures that you remain competitive and relevant in your field.

On-Going Education

Even if your state doesn't require it, on-going education will help you continuously improve your services and add new ones as well. Your professional growth and knowledge are both key to creating a sustainable business in this industry.

Client-Centric Services

By learning about your client base and understanding their needs, you can tailor your services to provide maximum value. This client-centric approach not only satisfies your customers but also helps in building trust and long-term relationships.

Continuous learning is important as it ensures you stay updated with changing regulations, industry trends, and the needs of your client base, allowing you to provide high-quality services. By expanding your knowledge and skills, you may also open up new opportunities and income streams, which will contribute to your long-term success and growth.

Secret #4: Work-Life Balance

We want to remind you that true success is not just about business growth and financial gains. It is about balance—the harmony between your professional life, personal well-being, and family or social life.

As you venture into your notary and loan signing agent career, it's important to understand that maintaining a healthy work-life balance is crucial for your long-term career success.

The Art of Self-Care

In the fast-paced world of notary and loan signing agent services, it's easy to get caught up in the whirlwind of work. However, consider this: Taking time for self-care can actually boost your productivity, creativity, and overall well-being. It's not a luxury; it's a necessity.

Here are some ways you can insert breaks and self-care into your busy schedule:

- **Routine breaks:** Implement regular breaks in your daily schedule. Short, frequent pauses allow you to recharge and refocus. When doing administrative tasks, try the Pomodoro Technique: Work for 25 minutes, then take a 5-minute break.
- **Exercise:** Incorporate physical activity into your routine. Whether it's a morning jog, yoga at lunch, or an evening walk, exercise keeps you healthy and mentally sharp.
- **Living mindfully:** Meditation and mindfulness practices are excellent ways to clear your mind. Even just a few minutes can do wonders for your mental clarity.
- **Weekend unplug:** Designate at least one day of the week as a "no work" day. Disconnect from work-related emails and calls. Let clients know about your day off by listing it prominently on your website, social media, and email communications. Reply to any messages or emails promptly the next day.

- **Plan getaways:** Regular vacations or staycations are essential. These breaks help you recharge and come back to work with renewed energy.

Outsourcing and Delegation

You don't have to do it all. Outsourcing and delegating tasks can free up your time and reduce stress. Here's when and how to consider hiring help for your notary and loan signing business:

- **Administrative Assistant:** Once your schedule fills up, you may want to consider hiring an administrative assistant for tasks like appointment scheduling, recordkeeping, and managing your calendar. They can also take calls and answer emails while you're fulfilling your notarial duties. This will streamline your workflow and provide you with valuable support.
- **Freelance Marketer:** If marketing is not your strong suit, it may make sense to outsource your marketing to a freelance marketer. Freelance marketers can develop a comprehensive digital marketing strategy tailored to your specific business needs. If you don't have a website or online presence yet, freelance marketers can build your website and create social media profiles on your behalf. Once these are created, they can save you valuable time by managing these platforms for you. They can post engaging content and respond to comments, resulting in a consistent online presence that doesn't require any hands-on work from you.
- **Other Freelancers:** If you don't require consistent help, you can simply hire freelancers on an as-needed basis. You can hire affordable freelancers on platforms, such as Fiverr, to create a custom logo, write blog posts, make promotional videos, and so much more.

When you're ready to hire out tasks for your business, you can find many viable contacts on Upwork or Indeed. Be sure to properly vet potential candidates by assessing their qualifications, conducting interviews, and checking references.

Work-Life Boundaries

Creating a clear boundary between work and your personal life is essential. Here are some strategies you may want to implement:

- **Scheduled vacation days:** As a business owner, you have the flexibility to take vacation days when it suits you. Plan these well in advance and advise your regular clients that you will not be available during those times.
- **Regular work hours:** Establish fixed working hours and stick to them. Avoid the temptation to work beyond your schedule unless absolutely necessary.
- **Overtime considerations:** One of the challenges of working from home or being your own boss is that you may end up working very long hours without realizing it. If clients keep calling after hours or if you are continuously answering emails, you run the risk of burnout. Overtime should be the exception, not the rule. In a service-oriented business, the quality of work matters more than the quantity of hours worked.

Balance is the key that will unlock your full potential, bringing you the satisfaction, prosperity, and longevity you desire in a career. So, prioritize self-care, know when to delegate, and set healthy boundaries. Your journey to success is an ongoing adventure, and it's one you should savor every step of the way.

Secret #5: Love What You Do

Loving what you do is not just about satisfaction and enjoyment; it can also have a significant impact on the success of your business. Here are some things to keep in mind:

- **Authenticity:** If you love what you do and believe in the service you provide, you bring authenticity to your work. Your passion and genuine interest in your services shine through, and clients are more likely to connect with and trust you. People are drawn to professionals who are passionate about their work.
- **Personalization:** Your interests, hobbies, and unique strengths can be integrated into your business, setting you apart from the competition. Consider how you can tailor your services to your personal interests. For example, if you're passionate about environmental issues, you could specialize in eco-friendly notarizations or help clients implement green document management.
- **Long-term commitment**: Enjoying what you do creates long-term commitment and dedication. When your work aligns with your interests and values, you're more likely to persevere through challenges, continuously improve your services, and grow your business over time.
- **Positive client relationships:** Your enthusiasm for your work translates into positive client interactions. Clients appreciate the energy and passion you bring to your appointments. Happy clients are more likely to become repeat customers and refer your services to others.

Incorporating your strengths and interests into your notary public and LSA business is about making your work meaningful, exciting, and fulfilling. It adds a layer of personalization and a unique touch that can set you apart from the competition.

The message is clear: Love what you do, and your business will reflect that love, attracting more clients and creating long-term success. It's not just about the work; it's also about the joy and fulfillment it brings to your life and the lives of others.

While there is no instant recipe for success, when practiced consistently, the powerful strategies in this chapter will elevate your business to new heights.

But these secrets aren't just words on a page; they're the building blocks of your success. By integrating them into your notary and LSA business, you're well on your way to creating a thriving six-figure empire.

Let's put these secrets to work:

- **Believe in yourself.** First and foremost, believe that you can achieve your goals.
- **Set clear goals.** Define what success looks like for you. Whether it's reaching a specific income level, gaining a certain number of clients, or expanding your services, try to set clear, achievable goals. Having targets in mind gives you direction and purpose.
- **Take consistent action.** Success is not built overnight. It's a series of small, consistent steps in the right direction. Keep showing up, day in and day out. With each appointment, every client you talk to, and every networking opportunity, you're one step closer to success.

- **Embrace growth.** The world is ever-changing, and so is your industry. Embrace change as an opportunity for growth. As you master new technologies and adapt to shifting trends, you'll stay at the forefront of your field.
- **Stay persistent.** There will be challenges, setbacks, and moments of doubt. But it is during these times that your persistence is most critical. Stay focused on your goals, and don't let obstacles deter you.

You have all the tools, knowledge, and strategies at your disposal to build a remarkable notary public and LSA business. It's a journey, and like any great journey, it's filled with twists, turns, and trials. The road to success may not always be straightforward, but the pursuit of your dreams is what makes your achievements even more satisfying.

You Can Do It!

Congratulations on reaching the final pages of this book! You have embarked on a journey of discovery in preparation to step into the world of notary public and loan signing agents, and now you stand on the threshold of a new beginning.

Starting your own notary public and LSA business is a significant step, and the path ahead may seem daunting. But remember, every grand journey ever made started with a first step. The very fact that you have read this far is proof of your ambition and willingness to learn. Believe in your potential, for you have the power to transform your dreams into reality.

The notary and loan signing agent industry offers a realm of opportunities. From helping clients with their notarizations to playing a vital role in real estate transactions, the services we can provide are both essential and in demand. Every loan signing, every document notarized, and every satisfied client you serve is a step closer to realizing your full potential in this industry.

One of the most remarkable aspects of this business is that it's versatile and adaptable. You can mold it to fit your life, whether you're seeking a full-time career or a part-time endeavor. You have the flexibility to build a schedule that suits your needs and the choice to start small or expand your services as your confidence grows.

While the costs for starting a notary public and loan signing agent business are low compared to most entrepreneurial ventures, you'll still need some initial capital to get started. Don't let this deter you! As the saying goes: "You have to spend money to make money". If raising initial capital is a concern for you, be sure to check out our book, *The Insider's Guide to Business Credit Using an EIN Only*. It's designed as a companion resource to help you receive funding for your new business without putting your personal assets at risk.

Once you get started, the income potential in this industry is staggering. Through your dedication and persistence, you can reach heights you might never have imagined. The variety of services you can offer, the potential for repeat business, and the ability to expand your expertise will set you on a path to financial success. You have the power to build a profitable and fulfilling business, and the sky's the limit.

Notary publics and LSAs are often unsung heroes. They play an important role in legal and financial transactions, ensuring the integrity and authenticity of documents. By choosing this path, you become a guardian of trust and truth, an advocate for accuracy, and a key player in the lives of countless individuals. You provide a valuable service that goes beyond mere notarization; you provide peace of mind.

The journey you're about to undertake may involve challenges, uncertainties, and moments of self-doubt. There will be times when you question your choices. It's during these moments that you must remember this simple truth: You have the ability to succeed. Believe in yourself, your skills, and your unwavering determination.

The knowledge and strategies that we've shared with you in this book are just the beginning. As you venture into the world of notary public and loan signing agents, the learning process continues. Your commitment to growth and adaptability will set you apart and guarantee your success.

Always remember that you don't need to go at it alone. A supportive network can be a lifeline! Connect with fellow notaries and loan signing agents, seek out industry associations, and explore local business groups. The insights, advice, and camaraderie you gain from networking can be invaluable in your journey.

The time to begin is now! As you close this book and prepare to embark on your notary public and loan signing agent career, remember that today is the perfect day to start. Don't procrastinate; seize the moment. The sooner you begin, the sooner you can realize the dreams you hold in your heart.

We're immensely grateful that you chose to read this book. We hope it has been a valuable companion on your journey to becoming a notary public and loan signing agent. As a parting request, we would be honored if you could take a few moments to leave a review or rating on Amazon. Your feedback is a powerful tool to help other aspiring notaries and loan signing agents find this resource.

We wish you the very best in all your endeavors, and we look forward to seeing you achieve incredible success. You can do it!

If you'd like support on your journey to a successful notary public and loan signing agent business, you can sign up for our email list by going to ***boundlessbooks.ck.page/notary****. You'll receive* *occasional emails from us with tips, encouragement, new book releases, and more!*

Other Titles by Alyssa and Garrett Garner

Etsy Business Launch: The Complete Guide to Making Six Figures Selling on Etsy

Candle Making Business: How to Launch a Thriving Six-Figure Candle Business from Home

The Insider's Guide to Business Credit Using an EIN Only: Get Tradelines, Credit Cards, and Loans for Your Business with No Personal Guarantee

Resources

Alternate income opportunity: mobile exam proctors. (2014a, January 22). National Notary Association. https://www.nationalnotary.org/notary-bulletin/blog/2014/01/alternate-income-opportunity-mobile-exam-proctors

Andrews, G. (2023, August 29). *What is a notary signing agent?* Forbes. https://www.forbes.com/advisor/education/what-is-a-notary-signing-agent/

Become a successful immigration forms specialist with expert training from LAIA. (2023, February 8). Latin Immigration Association. https://latinimmigration.org/becoming-an-immigration-forms-specialist-your-guide-to-success/

Buy domain name - cheap domain names from $1.37. (2018). Namecheap. https://www.namecheap.com/

Buyapowa. (2023, February 11). *88% of consumers trust word of mouth.* Buyapowa. https://www.buyapowa.com/blog/88-of-consumers-trust-word-of-mouth/

Create a free website or blog. (2018). WordPress. https://wordpress.com/

Electronic signature, electronic notary, sign documents online. (2023). Docverify. https://www.docverify.com/

Elliot, G. (2022, September 20). *17 motivating quotes about reinventing yourself.* Inc.com. https://incafrica.com/article/peter-economy-17-motivating-quotes-about-reinventing-yourself

Email marketing software. (n.d.). Constant Contact. https://www.constantcontact.com/

Email marketing for online creators. (n.d.). ConvertKit. https://convertkit.com/

Farrel, A. (2021, May 28). *The pros and cons of becoming a notary.* ProperSign. https://propersign.com/the-pros-and-cons-of-becoming-a-notary/

Farrell, A. (2021, December 3). *Sole proprietorship vs. LLC: Which is best for notaries?* PropperSign. https://propersign.com/sole-proprietorship-vs-llc-which-is-best-for-notaries/

Field inspection offers additional income opportunities for notaries. (2013a, April 18). National Notary Association. https://www.nationalnotary.org/notary-bulletin/blog/2013/04/field-inspection-offers-additional-income-opportunities-for-notaries

Find a notary public, buy notary supplies, become a notary. (n.d.). Notaryrotary.com. https://www.notaryrotary.com/

Google my business. (2019). Google. https://www.google.com/business/

Grow your business: Serving court documents. (2013b, July 11). National Notary Association. https://www.nationalnotary.org/notary-bulletin/blog/2013/07/grow-your-business-serving-court-documents

A guide to notary travel fees across the United States. (2021, July 21). National Notary Association. https://www.nationalnotary.org/notary-bulletin/blog/2021/07/notary-travel-fees-across-united-states

Henderson Britt, S. (2020, October 2). *365 marketing quotes to keep you fired up all year.* Skyword. https://www.skyword.com/contentstandard/marketing-quotes/

How to become a notary.(n.d.-a). American Association of Notaries. https://www.notarypublicstamps.com/how-to-become-a-notary/

How much money can you make mobile fingerprinting. (n.d.-b). Loan Signing System. https://www.loansigningsystem.com/how-much-money-can-you-make-mobile-fingerprinting.html

How much a notary public loan signing agent can make per month. (2023, January 18). Loan Signing System. https://www.loansigningsystem.com/blog/how-much-a-notary-public-loan-signing-agent-can-make-per-month

How to notarize a document. (2022, November 4). Docusign. https://www.docusign.com/blog/how-to-notarize-document

How to renew a notary public commission. (n.d.). Sos.nd.gov. Retrieved October 9, 2023, from https://sos.nd.gov/notaries-public/how-renew-notary-public-commission.html

I-9 forms: What notaries need to know. (2014b, August 13). National Notary Association. https://www.nationalnotary.org/notary-bulletin/blog/2014/08/i-9-forms-notaries-need-to-know

Justia US Law. (2019). 2019 Kentucky revised statutes: Chapter 423 - notaries public and commissioners of foreign deeds :: 423.395 denial, revocation, or limitation of commission. (effective January 1, 2020). *Justia Law.* https://law.justia.com/codes/kentucky/2019/chapter-423/section-423-395/

Marketing platform for small businesses. (2022). Mailchimp. https://mailchimp.com

Mobile notary public directory, free notary listings. (n.d.). 123notary. https://www.123notary.com/

McCormick, K. (2022, January 18). *What is google my business & why do I need it?* Wordstream. https://www.wordstream.com/blog/ws/2020/06/08/what-is-google-my-business

National notary association. (2022). National Notary Association. https://www.nationalnotary.org/

Nethercott, R. (2017, May 22). *5 reasons why repeat customers are better than new customers.* Constant Contact. https://www.constantcontact.com/blog/repeat-customers/

Notaries earn extra income serving as a remote testimony witness. (2015, October 28). National Notary Association. https://www.nationalnotary.org/notary-bulletin/blog/2015/10/notaries-extra-income-remote-testimony-witness

Notarize online. Anywhere. Anytime. (n.d.). Notarize. https://www.notarize.com/

Notary public faqs. (n.d.). Sos.state. https://www.sos.state.co.us/pubs/notary/FAQ/duties.html

Ordering a notary stamp. (n.d.-b). American Association of Notaries. https://www.notarypublicstamps.com/notary-faqs

Paid advertising: Definition, benefits, types, and platforms. (2023, June 9). Shopify.

https://www.shopify.com/za/blog/paid-advertising

PandaDoc demo request form. (n.d.). PandaDoc. https://demo.pandadoc.com/

The Pavaso platform. (n.d.). Pavaso Inc. https://www.pavaso.com/

Renew or update your license: Notaries public. (n.d.). Dol. https://www.dol.wa.gov/
professional-licenses/notaries-public/renew-or-update-your-license-notaries-
public

Riva, M. (2023, September 13). *How much does it cost to start an LLC?* (2023).
MarketWatch. https://www.marketwatch.com/guides/business/cost-start-llc/

Self-Employment Tax (Social Security and Medicare Taxes). (2019). IRS. https://
www.irs.gov/businesses/small-businesses-self-employed/self-employment-tax-
social-security-and-medicare-taxes

7 reasons to open a business bank account. (2021, June 2). Accion Opportunity
Fund. https://aofund.org/resource/7-reasons-open-business-bank-account/

Sheldon, R. (2022, September). *What is pomodoro technique time management?*
WhatIs. https://www.techtarget.com/whatis/definition/pomodoro-technique

Signing Agent. (n.d.). Signingagent. https://www.signingagent.com/

Signing agent tip: How to make more than $50 per loan signing. (2020, July 21).
National Notary Association. https://www.nationalnotary.org/notary-bulletin/
blog/2020/07/signing-agent-tip-how-to-make-more-than-50-per-loan-signing

Tariq, R. (2023, August 25). *How to become a certified apostille agent.* Pac Signing
Notary.   https://www.pacsigning.com/how-to-become-a-certified-apostille-
agent/

10 frequently asked questions about LLCs. (2021, April 12). Forbes. https://www.
forbes.com/sites/allbusiness/2021/08/12/10-frequently-asked-questions-
about-llcs/

10 tried-and-true email marketing tactics that actually work. (2020, September 11).
Forbes.   https://www.forbes.com/sites/theyec/2020/09/11/10-tried-and-true-
email-marketing-tactics-that-actually-work

Tennessee notary member center. (n.d.-c). American Association of Notaries. https://www.tennesseenotary.com/members

Top 10 identity verification software solutions for 2023. (n.d.). SEON. https://seon.io/resources/comparisons/identity-verification-software-tools/

12 ways to make money as a notary. (n.d.-a). Loan Signing System. https://www.loansigningsystem.com/how-to-make-money-as-a-notary.html

24 tax write-offs for notaries and signing agents. (n.d.). Keepertax.com. https://www.keepertax.com/tax-write-offs/notary-signing-agent

Web hosting services crafted with care. (n.d.). Siteground. https://world.siteground.com/

Wilkins, T. (2023, February 23). *Businesses that need notaries.* 123notary. https://blog.123notary.com/?p=24860

Wix.com. (2016, December 31). Wix. https://www.wix.com/

About the Authors

Alyssa and Garrett are married entrepreneurs who have built successful businesses across multiple industries.

Over the years, they've discovered a practical and reproducible framework for building highly profitable businesses in a short amount of time. Now, their passion lies in teaching budding entrepreneurs how to escape the grind and find financial freedom doing what they love.

When they're not building their entrepreneurial empire, Alyssa and Garrett enjoy traveling, ballroom dancing, and Broadway shows.

Thanks for reading!